JUMP INTO THE UNKNOWN

MELANIE DOWNES

Ark House Press
PO Box 1722, Port Orchard, WA 98366 USA
PO Box 1321, Mona Vale NSW 1660 Australia
PO Box 318 334, West Harbour, Auckland 0661 New Zealand
arkhousepress.com

© Melanie Downes 2020

Unless otherwise stated, all Scriptures are taken from the New Living Translation (Holy Bible. New Living Translation copyright© 1996, 2004, 2007, 2013 by Tyndale House Foundation. Used by permission of Tyndale House Publishers Inc., Carol Stream, Illinois 60188. All rights reserved.)

Some names and identifying details have been changed to protect the privacy of individuals.

Cataloguing in Publication Data:
Title: Jump Into The Unknown
ISBN: 978-0-6488873-6-2 (pbk)
Subjects: Biography; Christian Living; Missions;
Other Authors/Contributors: Downes, Melanie

Design by initiateagency.com

Contents

Special Thanks vii

Forward ix

Introduction: INTO THE UNKNOWN 1

Chapter 1: WHAT NOW? 3

Chapter 2: UNDERSTANDING 7

Chapter 3: LIVES TRANSFORMED 9

Chapter 4: BEFORE WE BEGAN 13

Chapter 5: ISHMAEL AND MUSSA 16

Chapter 6: LOSS 22

Chapter 7: MUSSA 25

Chapter 8: BIRTH 28

Chapter 9: MOTO 30

Chapter 10: IN ACTION 32

Chapter 11: MAMA MERCY 36

Chapter 12: HELPING ROSE 38

Chapter 13: INSURANCE 40

Chapter 14: COUNTING THE COST 43

Chapter 15: GOD MOMENTS 46

Chapter 16: EASY MONEY 49

Chapter 17: THE FIRST CROCODILE STORY 51

Chapter 18: THE SECOND CROCODILE STORY 55

Chapter 19: NOT MY SON 59

Chapter 20: WAIT 62

Chapter 21: IDA 64

Chapter 22: POWER PLAY 67

Chapter 23: SING IT 69

Chapter 24: THE BLACK ROOM 71

Chapter 25: IT WAS JUST A RIOT! 73

Chapter 26: TRUST AND BLAME GAMES 77

Chapter 27: CUTE 79

Chapter 28: HOME 82

Chapter 29: THE CREST OF THE WAVE 85

Chapter 30: FAVOUR 87

Chapter 31: JARRED'S 10th BIRTHDAY 89

Chapter 32: BLIND BLESSINGS 95

Chapter 33: WELCOME 98

Chapter 34: INITIATION CELEBRATIONS 101

Chapter 35: ELEPHANTS 103

Chapter 36: BUZZ 105

Chapter 37: TESTING 107

Chapter 38: THE PRODIGAL SON 110

Chapter 39: CRY 112

Chapter 40: RAMADAN RANDOMS 114

Chapter 41: STRANGE 116

Chapter 42: NORMAL 121

Chapter 43: HASSAN 125

CONTENTS

Chapter 44: CHOOSING LIFE 128
Chapter 45: CONCERNS. 130
Chapter 46: FASTING 132
Chapter 47: TAKING ACTION 134
Chapter 48: BEING TOO BUSY IS VANITY! 136
Chapter 49: LISTENING. 138
Chapter 50: DISGUST 140
Chapter 51: STRENGTH 142
Chapter 52: WHAT I DON'T KNOW 145
Chapter 53: DREAMING BIG 148
Chapter 54: JUMPING AGAIN 152
Encore: BONUS STORIES. 156

Special Thanks

As much as this book is my story, none of it would be possible without the help of some incredible individuals. I am ever so humbled and grateful for the gift of these wonderful people in my life. "Groupies, fellow 'Jumpers', faithful friends and family! Thanks for allowing me to include you in the stories, thanks for your help editing and for your feedback and encouragement.

Tim, Jarred and Clayton Downes, Sharyn Werner, Barry and Lois Downes, Geoff and Joy Suess and Chris and Bronwyn Downes.

Ayatu and Ellen Laja, Beni and Lucy Bwana, Melyna Chimoyo Jussa, Grace Bakali, Dorika Selimani, Amina Edward, Yvonne Tawakali, Frank and Fatima Matola, Niziah Chisusi, Muhammed Kassim, Kassale, Wyindi, Kalimu Kassim, Boniface Chilembe, Hussain Lemani and Edward Milanzi.

Pam and Graham Keen, Robyn Hughes, Elizabeth Dymock, Ruth Peckman, Kath Beeck, Doug and Barb Miller, Keith and Christeen, Jeff Chan, Julie-Ann Bray, Jean-claude and Joyce Manirakiza, Mable Mgawi, Susanne Turner, Helen Lauridsen, Duné Du Plessis, Michelle Kuss, Debbie Kruegle, Lawrance and Kerrin Munro, Ryan and Dani Long, Colin Pfaff and Ann Derrick.

Forward

am one of the people that has had the privilege of walking alongside Mel for a small part of the journey that is shared in the following pages. I have witnessed some of the times Mel has jumped, and she has been there encouraging me to jump at times, too. One thing you should know about Mel is that she has no pretense, what you see is what you get. She is the kind of friend where you can sit at her kitchen table in whatever state you are in, in whatever state she is in, and you will laugh, cry, feel loved and meet Jesus in whatever way you are needing. Mel is one of the most genuine people I know and someone who truly values fun. She is also one of the bravest and most faithful women I know. Yet Mel knows her flaws and shortcomings well; Mel never claims to have the answer or have it all together. One thing that I think you will come to see through these pages is that she is always vulnerable and willing to let you see the real her and more importantly let you see God working in her. The following stories come from a heart and a life that has trusted God over and over again. Mel and her family know what it is to choose to cling to Jesus even when you don't feel like it, when everyone is telling you to let go, when you don't see him, when life is trying to rip you from his grip. Their faith has been tested, yet Mel (and her family) still choose to joyfully trust in Jesus and in his call to jump with him.

As you read this book, you will feel like you are sitting at the kitchen table with a good friend, hearing their heart, having your heart heard. You will see God at work not only in these stories but in your own heart. I encourage you to sit with the stories don't race through them. Allow yourself to feel uncomfortable, confused, to feel deep joy, sadness, frustration, fun and hope. Let God speak to you as you sit with a friend who gets it. Life is sometimes hard, sometimes fun, sometimes it is all things at once. But life is definitely an adventure and worth living when you jump with Jesus.

Elizabeth Dymock *BAgrS, MIntRel, MIntTrdComLaw.*

Introduction

INTO THE UNKNOWN

On the front cover of this book is a photo of my two sons and their mates jumping off a jetty into Lake Malawi. I love this picture. It is the perfect example of freedom, of living life to the full and embracing all that you are. It is exotic. It is life-giving. It is fun! You can see the boys aren't particularly looking at each other they are focusing on what they are doing, yet they are loving jumping together. When they were little I would stand right next to them holding their hands coaxing them to be brave. Now that they are teenagers and have jumped so many times before, they hold nothing back. They are confident and strong because they have learnt how to jump properly.

Have you ever taken a leap of faith without knowing if you'll land well or not? It's the perfect empowering self-belief practice that is all about positive thinking and risk-taking. But that is not what I'm talking about.

My advice in this, don't jump unless you know Jesus. If you don't know him, you are going to crash and burn. The jumping is not the problem. It's the heartache that happens when you don't land properly, or the one you thought would catch you didn't.

It leaves a fear that can direct the rest of your life. Time doesn't heal in this type of hurt, it just makes you cynical, bitter and miserable. Life becomes difficult, it's much harder to live when you're wounded and you don't know the Healer.

However, if you know Jesus, he promises that he will never leave you. He'll jump right next to you and catch you before you land. He's planned it all anyway. He's jumped before and gives you direction about how to jump, what style to use, where to look, who to trust and how to land. It's the most magnificent rush you can imagine.

But hang on because not everyone feels this way. How is it that if you're about to jump, you can expect to face opposition, people telling you not to jump? You begin to doubt, you begin to lose your nerve and fear creeps in? You lose focus, suddenly smooth becomes rough, easy becomes hard. It can feel like you're standing unprotected on the edge of the precipice.

Life lessons tell you to hide, take cover or even better don't venture out at all, don't jump. Stay safe, don't make yourself vulnerable and you won't get hurt. But is not getting hurt enough motivation to stay safe? What happens if you do get hurt? Do you simply leave the uncleared path and walk away? Can you do that without something dying inside? Becoming a shell of a person who was once full of passion with a burning fire inside?

This story is one of someone who did jump, who jumped out into the middle of Africa. It was nothing to do with how strong I was, but everything to do with how strong Jesus is. I'm compelled to tell these stories because jumping can be a lonely road. A road we are told to walk on. However others are on it and when you meet them, they stay your friends for life because they understand. They've got your back and they'll push you to stay the course. They will jump wholeheartedly right next to you. We can all learn from their stories.

I love these folk, they are my kind of people, they are standing on the cliff, ready to jump, ready to go out into the unknown. You can trust these people with your life, you can hold their hand and they won't let go. They've jumped before, listen to them.

So let's do this. Put ourselves out there. It's not just jumping off a cliff or exploring deepest darkest Africa. It's more profound than that. God wants us all to take a leap of faith into the unknown. He wants us to learn from each other, to be inspired and motivated. God has called you and in his faithfulness, he will do it. With him you can jump!

Chapter 1

WHAT NOW?

Malawi

So there I am, sitting in a room and everyone has stopped talking and are just staring at me. It is awkward, I don't know a soul and they don't know me. They know my friend who invited me and that's who is being questioned. Who is the white woman? I know they are asking questions but I don't understand what they are saying. It would be years before I would know what these ladies are saying outside of me interpreting their looks and body language. I'm like the beacon on a hill, the nasty pimple on the end of a teenager's nose.

There was nothing I could do but sit and smile thinking 'how on earth did I get here?" A question that I know the answer to: I've spent the last three years getting to this very place, to this very place of awkwardness. I wasn't blending in at all but I was trying hard. I was wearing the headscarf (which is really not very flattering), I had my arms covered with a long-sleeved shirt, I was wearing the appropriate three layers of skirts: petticoat, skirt and a chitenji (like a sarong) over the top, not the most helpful attire in the tropics. I was sitting with my legs straight out in front of me and my back straight, apparently only one of two socially appropriate and comfortable positions for women to sit. But I was not blending. I felt like and looked more like a 'try-hard' pretending to be someone I was not. I was not a Yawo woman, I was an Aussie girl. I was not 5 foot and dark-skinned and it was not comfortable to sit like this. I was 6 foot and white, and I could not touch my toes on a good day. How was this combination ever going to work? What could I possibly offer these women who had never been this close to a white woman, who had never even seen one let alone have one in their house?

There were stories of white people and what they do. Eating children was one of them, casting spells, ruling with an iron rod and bathing in money were some other ideas. I was not really considered a person, more of a being out of some kind of fairy tale. I was an animal in a zoo to be looked at. Today I'm not the tourist but I'm in the cage having my photo taken by dozens of eyes.

The house was hot, really hot, 40 plus degrees Celsius. I was sitting on a grass mat on the hardened mud floor. There was one window but it was blocked up by bricks. The roof was made of grass with black plastic lining it. I could see it periodically rustle and something made its way under it. It took me several hours of watching. Rats had made this plastic their home.

The funeral outside continued but I could only hear a muffled whining sound of someone talking. I assumed this is the mosque leader. The men are about 100metres away from the women. The body of the deceased was in the house with me. I know this because if I moved another few centimetres over I'd be sitting on it. It had been washed and prepared in the traditional ceremonial way. The house was packed with women. I was touching people on every side and had been this way since this morning. The hours had passed by and I really didn't know what time it was, this was a timeless moment. Things had been the same way here for hundreds of years. I was the only different component. The only marker in time that says it was now and not then.

It was Ramadan, so everyone was fasting, there would be no food today, not even any water. I was feeling deliriously tired having sat for this long. I'd spent most of my time praying, asking God to do something here, because I was in trouble. I was so thirsty that I had no more spit in my mouth. I was dizzy from lack of food. I didn't really decide to fast today. It has been sort of forced upon me. No one was eating, there was no food.

WHAT NOW?

I gave myself some respite by asking several times if there was a bathroom. My gestures were having to get rather graphic until someone finally understood what I was wanting. I was taken to a little grass fence about one meter round, with a hole in the middle of it. Someone had 'fixed' the hole several times so that it was about 4 feet off the ground. Oh how I wished anyone of my Aussie girlfriends were with me. We'd laugh until it ached. But I was alone, the funny side lost in my problem-solving desperation. Climbing, balancing, straddling like an acrobat, I got the job done. As I was about to leave, I had a brilliant thought. I've had a water bottle hidden in my bag for the last 4 hours. Wishing I'd packed more than 500mls, I secretly downed the whole thing, praying that no one was spying on me. If I was caught I would have had a lot of explaining to do. I searched through the rest of my bag and found an old mint covered in lint. Rescued, thank you, Lord!

I was back in the house again. The brightness of outside rendered me blind in the darkness, I was trying not to stand on the bodies below me but it was near impossible. Ladies were laying out everywhere. The floor was covered; some were sleeping, others sat staring into nothing. That was until I entered. Now they stared at me. I sat back down in the silence that was only broken by the moans of the grieving; the funeral went on.

I heard a movement outside, something was happening. The door was opened, the body was taken away and the entire house erupted in wails and screams. It was terrifying; women were standing up and then throwing themselves on the ground. Others were trying to hold them up without success. I backed myself into a corner, the emotion of the room overwhelmed me. So much so that I started crying too. Silent tears ran down my cheeks. Not because I was grieving for the dead who didn't know, but I was certainly grieving.

This was my new life. This is what God had called me to do. To be the first to break the norm, this was to be the first of hundreds of funerals I would attend. These were to be the friends I was going to make and share the next season of my life with. I was grieving all that I'd left behind back in Queensland, back in another world, another time, another life.

The nine hours spent at that funeral that day was my entry into the world of ministry with the Yawo in Malawi. It was my insight into a world known by very few outsiders. I had landed in a place of vulnerability. The passion of God's calling on my life was taking me way out of my comfort zone. My ability to connect with these ladies and survive in this place was completely dictated by a willingness to jump.

Chapter 2

UNDERSTANDING

Malawi

A web of confusion was making our life so very difficult. There were so many layers of culture and history to unpack and understand. The Yawo, a particularly fascinating culture, was a hybrid of history that drew their behaviours from its layers of connections from the outside world dating back as far as time began. They were a very proud people group with thousands of years of traditions and beliefs who came to Malawi from Mozambique. There's a Yawo corridor that spans both countries. They were the money makers in their day, feared and powerful from a partnership with the Arab slave traders, capturing the neighbouring tribes and selling them on the slave market in Zanzibar off the Tanzanian coast. As a result of this connection, the Yawo became Muslim whilst the rest of the country is Christian. This is why the Yawo can be looked down upon, why they have been seen by others as primitively dangerous.

David Livingstone himself talks about the Yawo, two of his closest companions were Yawo men who took his heart back to England upon his death. With the abolition of slavery, the status of the Yawo plummeted from princes to paupers. Resisting the schools, hospitals and churches set up by the Christians the subsistence farming Yawo clung to Folk Islam, combining traditional African religion with Islamic beliefs.

Malawi became a British protectorate. Desperate and vulnerable from the slave trade and the threat of war, England moved in allowing Malawi to shelter under its wings as a British Protectorate. It remained this way until Indepedence and Kamuzu Banda became it's first President. He was a strict dictator respected by the nation, Malawi (then known as Nyasaland) kept it's economy strong and provided for its people. Colonialism left its mark, the country was a confusing conglomerate of cultures.

When we arrived, to my horror, our compound workers referred to themselves as our slaves, our servants. Grown men on their knees before me. Two hundred years of suppression had taught them to do so. Flashes of Apartheid and the Klu Klux Klan danced before my eyes, it went against everything I stood for.

As we met some other expatriates we heard comments like, 'You can't trust Malawians", or "Don't let them in your compound", "Don't let your kids mix, they might catch something". Smiling nicely on the outside, rage bubbled up inside me. I could never live like this. I will never bark out orders nor I will never treat one human being anything less than another. Children are children. How could I discriminate against them because of their poverty, their skin colour, their suffering?

I was told that this was the system, and I must live in it. We were to study language and culture. Historically only Tim would be expected to go out into the villages, I was the homemaker and learning the language was probably out of my reach. Most expatriate women stayed at home, teaching their children and ventured out only to go to the capital city or the lake. If ever anything was going to offend me this was it. It was like they were waving a red flag before the bull. The fire inside me raged. What is wrong with this place? What is wrong with these people? I felt like Jesus in the temple, I was going to have to make a whip and blaze a new trail. It was going to be the hardest journey of my life, but I'd already made the jump, there was no looking back now.

Chapter 3

LIVES TRANSFORMED

Malawi

When we looked into the Yawo culture it didn't take long for us to realize that we were living in a male-dominated Islamic community. Women spent most of their time working hard in the fields of buying/selling in the market. We meticulously studied the culturally appropriate behaviours and interactions of how Yawo men and women related to each other. Women generally laid low, took the more respectful background role and let the men take the lead. They didn't always initiate greeting, they knelt before their husbands and other men and never interrupted or showed assertiveness in public.

It didn't take long for us to figure out that this outspoken, liberated Aussie girl was going to have to change if we were to gain trust, respect, credibility and friendship in this community. It was a scary insight to realise how quickly my best aspirations to help could be instantly destroyed by ignorant friendliness. We were coming into Malawi on the back of 200 odd years of historical colonialism. As a typical Australian woman I was going to have to reinvent myself if I was to get anywhere in this community!

It was best if I didn't give Tim an instruction in public, never interrupted him if he was speaking, never spoke publicly in a group if there were men nearby. I was to be seen but not heard, I was to watch where I looked, keep my eyes averted, not give anyone cause to think that Tim was anything but the man of our household. Everything I'd ever been taught was being tested. It certainly put a strain on our marriage.

After about 18 months of 'playing the game' as I like to call it, I won the jackpot! I was invited to meet some of the wives of the Yawo workers on our team. I pounced at the opportunity of spending most afternoons visiting women, getting to know them and their kids. Being starved of friendship Jarred (5), Clayton (3) and I would just hang out in the village. (Not such a light-hearted decision as one in five children die here from disease.) I had to trust God to protect my babies as we made ourselves vulnerable as I was desperate for a connection in the community. It was essential to us being here, it was God holding me steady, as I jumped with my limited language into the hidden lives of those living in the background.

These quiet attempts of connection, however, came with a rather rude fanfare. We were a novelty, drawing a crowd where ever we went. The cry would go out. 'She's got kids, there are Asungu (foreign) kids'. Jarred and Clayton were the first white children many people had ever seen. I was interesting but they were fascinating. Toddlers at the time, Jarred and Clayton had no idea what all the fuss was about. They were colour blind; screaming at strange people if they got too close, fighting for a toy they wanted to play with, happy to be where ever Mum was. They would follow my lead. If I was contented so were they. If I wasn't the real deal, these women would see through me in a heartbeat. Already these new relationships were under trial. One of my friends got so tired of the crowds and seeing my boys distressed she had her teenage sons stand on guard with big sticks, barking orders and throwing rocks into the pressing crowd.

As these precious friendships grew I started to understand the problems and frustrations many women faced. I offered to pray and tried to help without creating dependency (a challenge in a poverty-stricken community!). My judgments however were often offbeat. I'd see children dressed in rags and be thinking to myself how I could share some of my children's clothes, only to hear my friend brag how her children are well dressed in the community. I'd feel compassion for the small tomato stallholder selling 30 delicately placed produce, only to have my friend tell me about her better income-generating activities. I was the learner in the situation. They were helping and guiding me with their local wisdom. I was simply out of my depth and they were teaching me to swim. My understanding of what was important had to change, contentment and wealth can be two very different things.

Yawo society is matrilineal, meaning that family lines are traced through females rather than males (patrilineal). A mother and her daughters would stay together while husbands moved from their home village to live with their wives. Husbands commonly divorced their wives and sadly, could not always be relied upon. Having multiple wives was commonplace. The kids had their aunties and grandmothers tending fields, keeping the family fed and clothed and caring for them in the face of poverty, oppression and tragedy.

To my delight, I discovered most women had strong networks and connections. The sisterhood, despite appearing subservient and meek, was very strong, much stronger than I could have imagined. They lived under oppression and organized themselves so that they could help each other in times of need. These groups provided a natural process of gathering for support. An unwritten rule of I'll scratch your back now, if you'll scratch mine tomorrow. I was to find out where my place was in all this. What kind of back-scratching was I to do? How were any of them ever going to be able to scratch mine? It was a steep learning curve for me to connect and share with others and a very hard group to crack into. It took a long time for me to feel an accepted outsider.

In time a group of us were meeting regularly at different family homes. We'd talk about life and share our issues. God would often come into the conversation and I'd be able to explain what I knew about issues relating to family and marriage, God's promises to his children. It was radically liberating for us all. Learning a new narrative strengthened us. Nothing was wasted as knowledge was not something openly shared in a Yawo village; possessions, yes but knowledge, no. Each woman and her family were on their own journey of discovering the freedom they could have; the original plan God wanted them to understand. Although I'd come in from another direction, I was now very much on this same road.

I loved that these ladies were not reliant on me; they'd continue to meet if I was not there. The women were listening to God's Word and incorporating it into the Yawo context. They'd gather an offering each week to use in times of emergency or tragedy and they'd give counsel to other women in their communities. I was learning so much from them about the needs of the Yawo and the crippling effect Westerners can have with some misdirected good intentions. I was not the Great White Saviour in a pith helmet like the famous explorer David Livingstone. It was far better for me to be a humble guest, welcomed by their generosity.

This one circle of friends had powered on for years and the sphere began stretching further afield. Tim worked with five other groups around the region. He faithfully taught God's Word and we could see it taking root and changing lives. The success of friendships made in our women's group had given us insight into how to best love the women in other groups.

As I reflected on my experience and Australian traditions, I could see how God had prepared me for this. There were unifying qualities all women had. We needed to love and be loved, we needed a purpose and we needed to belong. My pride and liberation would have to take a back seat, as I had to forego my rights and align my behaviour with those around me. This was a brutal process. But I couldn't exactly go around complaining. I was committed, I'd made the jump. I was living in their country so I had to learn to do it their way.

The steep learning had me navigating my own cultural assumptions and responsibilities. It opened the door to a whole new world of opportunities. Of course, I was still an Aussie girl! I made sure Tim knew that when I sat at his feet, or asked him for money to buy food for the family, I was 'playing the game'! Yet he had graciously learnt how to make things easier for me and was aware of what was necessary to gain and maintain respect and trust in the community. Oh and I still let him know when this Aussie girl is not happy!! He doesn't have to guess!

Chapter 4

BEFORE WE BEGAN

Australia

You might think that as soon as you agree to jump that a beam of light shines down from heaven and everything you touch turns to gold. I'd like that too. But what really happened was the opposite. When we were back in Australia, I watched as Tim answered a call from the Director of our organization. He asked if we would consider going to Malawi, Africa on a long-term basis. By the look on Tim's face, I thought someone had died. We'd always said that if God was going to call us into full-time ministry he'd have to back us into a corner and strike us by lightening. As it turns out, this phone conversation was the lightning bolt that would change our lives.

The Bible talks about the peace of God that transcends all understanding. And although it wasn't in the form of a dove, we both felt the Spirit of God physically. A confidence that was so rock solid there wasn't a doubt that this was from God. My head was spinning and my emotions shot, but in my heart of hearts, I knew that the answer was yes. We were to take our then two-year-old and our unborn baby to Africa to reach the Yawo. This was going to be outright obedience because if I allowed my logic and my reasoning to take control, this was a really dumb idea! Even then little did I know just how incredibly impossible this calling was going to be. It was like the floodgates of opposition opened and we were standing in the middle of the river!

We'd been part of a home group. An awesome group of young adults that were really asking big questions about life and calling. We'd kind of inspired each other to ask God what he wants from us and what should we be doing with our lives. We were following the 40 Days of purpose written by Rick Warren and it was challenging all of us.

Tim and I were already very committed to serving as a Builder and a Teacher. We'd both grown up with parents in full-time ministry serving amongst Indigenous Australians, Tim starting in the Northern Territory on a community up in Arnhem Land and me in the coastal communities of Queensland. We knew what cross-cultural work looked like. We knew what it was to rely on God, we didn't see it through rose coloured glasses, there was no glamour involved. We weren't out there trying to prove ourselves and certainly didn't want the 'spiritual limelight' of standing on a pedestal. We were quite happy serving God in Cairns Queensland building and teaching.

However, there was a restlessness that was growing in our hearts. Some days whilst driving home from work we'd be asking ourselves, is this it? Is this what we do for the rest of our lives. To settle down into our jobs, raise our kids, pay off our house and go through the motions until we were old and frail? Most of the time I was very happy to live this kind of life, but sometimes in the quiet moments, I got the feeling that there was going to be more out there for me. I was going to have to take a break and do something a bit different. My ideas and plans, however, were nothing like what God had in store for us.

Being called to serve in Malawi was definitely not what I had in mind. I knew what cross-cultural missionaries were like; most very sensible and practical people, living a life of hardship and not always relevant to their home culture as they surrender all in service in some faraway place. I certainly was not keen to put my hand up or jump up and down to volunteer to go to some leper colony to be one! Tim and I were on the same page with this. So when I looked at his face that Sunday night I knew that what we were about to do wouldn't make a whole lot of sense! God promises a peace that surpasses understanding, which is really fortunate, because otherwise I would have been a lot like Jonah and running the other way.

    The first big hurdle was when we announced our calling to our family. They were in shock. They all thought we'd gotten travel out of our system several years before when we'd taken 12 months off and backpacked around the globe. That was supposed to be our adventure. This was supposed to be the season of producing grandchildren and settling down. Our church family wasn't much different, as they'd planned for Tim to become their youth pastor. It had been voted on and everything! It pained us to break these expectations and watch the trust of our precious friends be tested as we explained what God had but on our hearts.

Chapter 5

ISHMAEL AND MUSSA

Malawi

Two young local boys lived across the dirt road opposite our house in Malawi. They lived in a small two-room mud hut with a grass roof in an open field. At that stage, they had a mother and father living with them as well as an older brother and two younger brothers. The names of these two boys were Ishmael and Mussa.

Ishmael was quiet and reserved and Mussa walked around with a huge smile on his face. Tentatively they came to visit and we invited them to play with our boys Jarred and Clayton who at that time were 2 and 4 years. We learnt that although Jarred towered over his new friends Ishmael and Mussa were both in fact older five and seven years respectively. A lack of nutrition in their diet had stunted their growth.

These boys became part of a new neighbourhood gang that met in our backyard to play. Sometimes numbering up to 20 kids at a time, we explored the style of play that happens when you combine children from different cultures. A new institution was created in our compound over the years. It was the key to Jarred and Clayton surviving in this harsh climate. A group of friends established to love and accept each other in a way few others have done before. It would carry us through the worst of experiences.

We watched as Ishmael and Mussa's parents separated and left the area. The boys always returned daily to play despite the fact they slept kilometres away. Later we found that they were sleeping at different houses each night as Mum found new boyfriends who didn't appreciate their company. The boy's father was not the most reliable person either. We suspected some mental health issues existed in his life.

There were many Mexican standoffs (or should I say Malawian standoffs) with Ishmael and Mussa's family. We refused to let them live with us; their parents needed to take responsibility for them. We nursed and cared for these boys but would hunt down their father to take the boys to the hospital. I remember one day waiting with Ishmael, who, feverish with malaria, convulsed on the ground. He was unconscious as we sorted out a family member (mother, father, aunty grandmother, anyone would do) to help take him to the hospital. We maintained that as much as we loved these boys we could not take sole responsibility for them.

Things deteriorated with their family, Grandma was put in charge of the boys. She was an elderly woman barely able to sustain herself. A thin gaunt slither well into her 70's she was, in fact, the boy's great grandmother, a woman outliving her relatives by decades. She eked out her existence by subsistence farming. She ate what she grew. There was rarely any money in the household and they were often hungry for several months of the year. Grandma lived 20 kilometres out of town.

After not having seen the boys for a while, one day Ishmael turned up with Mussa not far behind. The boys were obviously exhausted. They didn't knock on our door, but just sat under the patio quietly. We gave them water and waited for them to speak. They were fighting back tears.

"They don't want us," he sobbed, "nobody wants us." The boys had left their grandmother's village hut early in the morning after having spent another night without food in their stomachs. Grandma, out of sheer survival, had stopped feeding them. If she gave away her food she would starve. She sent them back to their mother.

Their mother had a new boyfriend. This guaranteed food for herself and her unborn child. They had gone to her only to be rejected under threats and abuse.

They could not find their father and had wandered the maze of villages in an attempt to find their aunty who again refused to care for them with already too many mouths to feed. Ishmael and Mussa were skinny, malnourished and tired. They had sores all over their bodies, scabies and boils, their eyes were dull and their spirits were low.

We enquired further and then allowed the boys to rest and eat some food we provided. They at least would be safe for the next 10 hours until evening. Our home had become a safe haven for many children. A place where kids could come and know they are loved and cared for. A place of fun that was free from fear. We made the rules very clear. Children were welcome only if we knew their parents. We allowed playtime from 2pm to 5pm giving kids enough time to get home before darkness set in. All our local workers enjoyed this new regime. Our compound (backyard) represented a place of healthy community.

In Yawo culture, when a serious problem was faced, a 'Magambo' or court case was called. People significant to the issue were gathered and the problem discussed in a very formal way. We learnt that the protocol of such meetings needed to be studied and conducted ceremoniously. They were integral to being accepted into the community.

The court case regarding the wellbeing of Ishmael and Mussa was opened. Two senior compound workers were invited as well as the family members and village representatives. We waited with our compound workers realizing that no one from the community wanted to own the problem of these two boys. The answer had been given in their absence. We began the meeting anyway.

The boys explained the story again each getting a turn to speak. It was difficult to hear little Mussa through his excessive stuttering. The more nervous he was the worse he would stutter. A time of silence gave our workers a moment to process the story and give a response. A response we were not ready for. Our hearts were soft towards these two boys, they had nowhere to go, and they were hungry, tired and suffering. We were expecting compassion, what we heard was far from it.

"Stop crying, and man up. " An English version of what was said. "Stop feeling sorry for yourself and make a plan. Fight and keep working hard. If you don't you will die. Do you hear me?"

Tim and I were dumbfounded. How could they be so harsh to such little children? The meeting finished and we let the boys play while we continued to talk things through with our local employees. We were to find somewhere for these boys to stay for the night until a better solution was found.

It was explained to us that children die all the time if they give up. Attitude is everything. There are no safety nets. These children need motivation to work, not compassion to give up hope. It was a steep learning curve for us, a rude shock.

Our Gardener took the boys until we tracked down their father. He agreed to take them, at least for now. Another woman living opposite us, was wealthy and respected in the community. She organized a house for them to live in rent-free. It was very rundown, with a giant hole in the roof and walls disintegrating but it was safe. We enjoyed visiting and giving some basic gifts, blankets, clothes and mosquito nets. The boys were delighted. Their father was employed as a part-time worker, digging holes and slashing grass for our compound. We thought this was a wonderful solution.

It lasted for at least a year until Ishmael's father went missing. We found out through their neighbour, a friend of mine who already had 7 children of her own. She had taken the boys in and had given them food and ensured they were safe at night. She came to me after a week. "Mama, I cannot keep looking after these boys. We cannot let them sleep in that house alone, someone or something will take them". (Children often disappear at night due to child trafficking or wild animals.) The risk was too high. I gave her some food and asked her to look after the boys for a little longer. I always fed them snacks during the day as they played and at least they were getting porridge at night. We needed to find their parents.

Eventually we tracked down their mother. She was waiting to give birth in the local hospital. Sleeping in the open hospital courtyard next to the gutter as the maternity ward was overflowing. The water trickling down the gutter was rancid and my stomach turned as I spoke to her. She explained it was too hot to stay inside with too many people, constant noise and lights that never went out. She would rather risk malaria from the mosquitos than go any longer sleeping under the bed she was assigned to, while she waited for her unborn child to come. (Beds are only for mothers who have had their babies. Waiting mothers are to sleep on the floor.)

She was aware that her children were abandoned but there was very little she could do. She already had two other boys she was caring for, and even then she was risking rejection from her new boyfriend/husband. His baby she was carrying was her hope of security and longevity with him. I understood and we prayed together over the situation. There clearly was little she could do, the fear in her eyes told me her desperation. (I was with her when she later had the baby, a little girl. Unusually she was born with 12 fingers and 12 toes.)

We managed to track down the father who turned up with the boys in tow. He was very upset with me and demanded I took care of his kids. He only stayed a minute and then was gone again. I was left at a loss. I went in search of advice from my local friends. It all pointed in the same direction. "Be careful Mama, this will get you into a lot of trouble." Child trafficking was very common and I was at risk of having these children in my care for a long period. I could be wrongly accused and end up in jail. They were not my children and those who had been helping had little left to give.

It was obvious I needed to jump but where, how? The answer led me to the local child welfare office. Yes, it was the first time I had ever heard that there was such a place. I went with my friend. It was a positive meeting and the officer was quick to take action. He gathered two policemen, myself and my friend and the two boys. We went in search of their father. It was a horrible saga that left me full of mixed emotions. I was relieved at finding the right authorities but concerned at the line they took. Ishmael's dad was remarried and his new wife was shaking in her boots. The father sat silent and furious at us. How dare I, a woman, report him. I consoled myself that at least, I was safe with the authorities. The last thing I needed was to be accused of child trafficking.

The boys went back to stay with their father and things seemed to settle down for a while. They still regularly came to play each day. Jarred and Clayton enjoyed their friendship. Each year we would measure the children's height on our outside veranda posts. Every year most children grew about 10 cm. This was a point of real pride for them to have their names and heights recorded for others to see. This was great, except for Ishmael and Mussa struggled to grow 5cm. I worked hard at giving them enough food to keep them healthy without creating dependency; a very fine line.

Chapter 6

LOSS

Malawi

Not long after Ismael and Mussa went back to their father I became extremely sick with malaria. I was wracked with fevers, every joint felt ready to break apart. As my friends came to visit me, several explained that sickness was a result of my actions with the child welfare. They believed that Ishmael and Mussa's Dad had cursed me and I was being punished. We gathered our friends and prayed. The fever lifted and I recovered not long after. We remained diligent in our prayers of protection.

Years went by and the boys were passed from one family member to another. No one was willing to take them long term, but all of them were afraid to abandon them completely in fear of being reported. The boys spent many hours on the streets waiting outside our front gate until they were allowed in our compound. On our first home assignment, it was reported to us that Ishmael and Mussa waited every day for 10 months at our front gate, hoping for our return.

It makes me wonder whether this contributed to Ishmael's behaviour, as something happened within him that made matters a lot worse. I guess years of rejection will make a person do all sorts of things. Ishmael became distant and we would see him hanging around with other boys much older than him. He was living across the road from us for a while with my neighbour who had helped them out years ago. She wanted to give him a chance, but was forced to make him leave when he began to steal. Stealing became a way of life for

Ishmael. He began with little things, matchbox cars, toys our boys would leave in the yard, petty things that really didn't matter. He knew very well what we thought about stealing. He would often confess and ask for forgiveness. He still came regularly to play.

For years Jarred would say Ishmael was his best friend. He certainly was his most faithful friend and the boys played well together. Ishmael was 3 years older than Jarred and although they were the same height, he had learned a lot more about the rawness of life than Jarred. We forbid Ishmael from talking to Jarred about the sexual training he had during his initiation ceremony. We explained that Jarred had to wait until he was initiated before he could hear such things, a culturally appropriate loophole that would protect our boys for a little while.

Ishmael spent less time with us and more time with the teenage boys wandering the streets. He began to dress differently. He had always worn the clothes we supplied; now he was wearing new items we had ever seen before. He wore his pants halfway down his backside showing his underwear. Ishmael had become a part of a local gang who called themselves. "Niggers" We still let him into our yard, but generally Mussa came alone. Ishmael would appear for a few minutes and then was gone.

Finally one day we noticed money, an iPod and finally Tim's phone were all gone. Ishmael was stealing from us. He finally was caught and the items were found. We chose not to involve the police. Instead Tim tried a rehabilitation program where he came and worked three times a week on our trial farm in an attempt to rebuild trust. It didn't work. He helped himself to our office supplies right under our noses. His clear lack of fear was evident. We had to take the matter to the police. He was arrested and beaten in the local jail. Tim advocated for his release. The mandatory sentence was 8 years, way too long for a 14-year-old boy.

We thought this would end the matter and grieved the loss of our friend. Ishmael was no longer allowed in our compound. Jarred was shattered, "What did I do wrong Mum?" Betrayal drifted through the whole compound. Mussa suffered most; he could no longer come to play, at the risk of losing his brother, his only consistent companion.

Months went by and the boys continued to play with their other friends. It just wasn't the same. One day the boys were all playing hide and seek when they found Ishmael hiding behind the shed in our compound. More police and more warnings. We haven't seen Ishmael since.

Mussa however is another story. Desperate to stop the same thing from happening to Mussa I visited with his Mother. She had moved on to another husband. We discussed the possibility of finding a permanent home for Mussa. The entire family including Dad, Aunty and Grandma were happy with this idea. The only problem was, how on earth was this going to happen? I began using all the contacts I had gained over the years, to work out options. Boarding schools wouldn't have him as he was now 11 years old and still in year 3.

Most people in our area were too poor or too worried about committing to care for Mussa. Tim and I prayed. It seemed we needed to look further afield to find a safe place for Mussa.

Child services do allow foster care arrangements in Malawi but they are not very proactive in sourcing them. After a lot of searching and word of mouth enquiries, I found a family who were willing to take him. The man worked for the Bible translation project we are involved with and he and his wife couldn't have kids. What a relief! We began to put things in place. I couldn't help everyone but for now, I was determined to help this one boy. The look of desperation in his eyes was motivation enough to jump again.

Chapter 7

MUSSA

Malawi

The road was completely blocked by a semi-trailer. Its brakes had obviously failed whilst winding up the narrow range road and the driver had jackknifed the rear end of the truck into the bank of the hill. One side dropping off to a cliff held the front cab and about ten men laying underneath surrounded by tools and rocks. I'm not quite sure what the rocks were for, perhaps as extra protection if the truck was to move.

There were about 100 or so people gathered on this normally lonely road. They had climbed the hill from the village below to join in the action. We were at a loss of what to do. I was in our car with Mussa, his Mother, little sister, cousin and Aunty along with the child protection guy who looked about 12 years old. This was our final journey to get Mussa an 'at risk' child, a safe place to live. We had found him a new foster family.

It was three days before our family was due to fly back to Australia for Home Assignment. Six months in Australia travelling and talking about the work in Malawi. We had to get Mussa sorted before we left. Amazed at how each step of the way doors opened, stepping through each time gave us hope that this actually might work out. An impossible task we had deemed it highly unlikely, but perhaps we were wrong.

We were taking Mussa to his new home after many months of searching and tactfully negotiating with government departments. We had already visited Mr Kassim and his wife and discussed the matter of them caring for this child. We had also gone to Mussa's family and discussed the arrangements. Mussa was to move and live with this new family. He could return during school holidays. His Mum was glowing, this was her big break. Her child was going to make it, she openly talked with me and her eldest son. "Perhaps Mussa will grow up to get a job that will look after us all?" We could only hope.

I sat quietly in the car and prayed. " Lord, how are we going to get past this truck? "

To the side of us was a guard rail, a steel barrier used to stop cars from going over the edge. Some local men had removed the bolts in one section and came to our window. They told us we could pass by the truck by going down the edge of the drop-off. They were very helpful but at a price. K1000 ($5, a lot of money here.). We watched as several cars went by us only to refuse to pay and turn around. We waited and prayed.

Suddenly my government department friend remarked, ' that's the DC' (District Commissioner) and jumped out of the car. Those men operating the guard rail scam immediately dropped the rail and the way opened. We drove in behind the DC precariously balancing off the side of the hill. Then it got worse. He was bogged. Dust was flying from behind his back tyres but he wasn't moving, we were stuck on the side of the drop off not being able to go forward or backwards. Our car was on such an angle I wondered if we were going to slide sideways. "Oh Lord please help!"

Several young guys pushed the DC's car. They edged forward enough to open a small gap in front; enough for us to squeeze through. I locked the car into 4WD and went for it. Lots of sliding and bouncing but we popped up onto the main road. We'd made it! Years of 4WDriving for fun in Far North Queensland came in handy.

We arrived at Mussa's new home and met his new family. It was surreal to see how happy everyone was about the arrangement. The government official was extremely surprised. This is not normal, he said. I praised the Lord for his help. With all the formalities completed, we drove home. My heart contented, Mussa was safe, wanted. He would eat every day and go to school. The impossible can happen when God is in control.

Chapter 8

BIRTH

Malawi

Oh dear Lord, help me. What do I do now? Should I remind you, God, that I am only a Health and Physical Education teacher, sporting a first-aid certificate at best? I was not trained for this! My friend looked at me again as her rescuer, she was on the bed, her body tight with pain. The contractions were seconds apart and I felt the anxiety building with each one.

I prayed with her quickly again, not really ending the prayer that just turned silently inside my head. Lord, help me find a nurse, a doctor, anyone who can deliver this baby other than me!

I walked out the door onto the concrete patio and waded through the mud to the nearby mango tree. I asked some ladies who are standing nearby. "Is the midwife around?"

Oh look, the Azungu speaks Ciyawo. I smiled for the thousandth time and agreed that my party trick was amazing. I greeted all those who came over to see, politely. Yes I spoke Ciyawo, wasn't that nice. Now, where was the nurse?

Oh there she was, she had just bought some fish from the river nearby. How lovely for her. Not wanting to be rude, I greeted her again (and yes again I spoke Ciyawo, it was amazing). Then asked ever so gently, would she mind coming to see my friend. Oh good; She will. Praise God.

We walked into the labour ward tracking mud from outside. My friend stood over a bucket relieving herself. (Yes women here can do this standing up.) As I quietly made my way out the door the nurse called after me. "Don't you want to stay and watch?"

"No thank you, this is your job, not mine!" I've never been good at watching such things. I certainly wasn't going to watch if I could help it! I sat on the bench outside and watched the bats fly out of the hole in the roof instead.

After some time, two ladies from the Ladies Group rounded the corner. Yay I was saved! We had company, support and someone other than me to wash the afterbirth out of the bed sheets! We sat in silence listening to my friend groan through clenched teeth. Five minutes later a wail echoed out. A baby girl!

Village ladies were extremely tough, they had to be; I was embarrassed to reflect on the pampering I had when I gave birth to our boys in Australia. We joked together how much a small baby could cause so much pain. A cow walked past the back door, but nobody noticed. We praised God all was well, each lady bowed her head and thanked him for the blessing of new life and prayed protection from the evil one. I signed myself out as the official guardian, said thanks to the nurse and headed for home.

Tim was sitting at the workers table near the garage when the men all greeted me. As I gave Tim the car keys, he asked what was wrong with my friend in the end. I don't normally leave Jarred and Clayton to fend for themselves at school. Surprised I frowned at Tim. "Didn't you know she was in labour? She was 7cm by the time we got to the hospital!"

Tim cringed, "Gee, if I'd known that I wouldn't have let her wait that long. I thought she had a sick kid or something."

This was the 5th birth I had attended in the last month. Little did I know at the time but that same year I was to attend 12 births in all. Many of my friends were pregnant and scared to go to the hospital, they would get ignored or abused. My white skin would come in handy when making sure my friends were attended to. I never saw my own children's birth, but I sure have been up close and personal with the action now. It had stretched me way beyond what I am comfortable with. But by the grace of God do we stand!

This was not going to be the last time I'd be in the hospital, perhaps God decided it was a good way to keep me humble and reliant on him.

Chapter 9

MOTO

Malawi

Moto means fire in Ciyawo, an essential part of everyday life. Almost everyone cooks on an open fire. (apart from us who cook on gas). Firewood is getting harder and harder to find. Charcoal is made and sold because it is easier to cook on but the forests and woodlands are thinning. Women have to walk further and further to gather firewood and carry it back to their homes in giant piles precariously balanced on their heads. I've tried doing this myself and it is ridiculously hard. The wood they are carrying easily matches their own body weight.

I've been camping many times in my life, I like cooking on open fires, barbeques are fun, but I have never considered fire an essential part of life, not like they do here in Malawi. Candles are still extremely common. With so many power outages, candlelit dinners are a regular occurrence even at our place. Malawi has enough electricity to supply only a fraction of the community who can actually afford it, and often we are paying for nothing.

'Moto, Moto' (Fire, Fire). The nearby mud hut burst into flames. The village group who had been in heavy discussion with Tim were suddenly on their feet ripping apart the mud hut. The owner of the house, an older woman grabbed her punga knife (machete) and was cutting into the strings that held the grass roof onto her house. 'Take it off' she cried.

It took Tim a while to catch on. There was no time for buckets of precious water, the people were just pulling the house apart, roof off, fences pulled down, kitchen annex dragged into open ground. If they got them away from the fire, then it would cause less damage. Smart, very smart. By the time the fire reached the top of the walls, it had nothing left to burn. Someone threw in a bucket of water and the whole saga fizzled out. The people had been through this kind of thing before and their savvy was impressive.

The group turned back to the meeting place, when a young boy about 10 emerged from the side of the hut. Face ashen and guilty. Suddenly the owner of the house appeared and gave the boy a swift clout around the ear. Clearly he was being blamed for starting the fire. He'd been playing with matches inside the house.

The boy disappeared for a minute then re-emerged with an axe swinging wildly in the air, wielding it at his mother. Mad as a hornet from being shamed in front of everyone, he charged. Baba Windi, who had been preaching with Tim, intercepted but the boy sidestepped and launched himself again. More people intervened and the chase began. Dodging and diving the boy was determined to vent his anger. Finally, someone was able to grab the axe and defuse the situation. The afternoon's entertainment died down. The group gathered again and sat in a time of silence and prayer. Putting faith into action was much more important than simply sitting around and talking about it. It constantly convicted us.

Rolling a faith teaching around to taste its flavour, to ponder it, discuss it and decide if it was delicious enough to saviour, is not part of life here. If God says it, then we do it. Just like they didn't hesitate when the house was on fire, new believers don't have the luxury of hesitating to see if they like a particular teaching or not. Living out God's word has to be real and practical, it has to make sense, it has to be applied right now. Academic language is a waste of time, philosophy isn't in vogue, we have to live everything we are teaching, we need to bring God's word into every aspect of life and act out what we believe.

Just like jumping, you don't need to know all the theories behind the different techniques, the history behind it or the stories of those who have jumped before you. You just need to do it.

Chapter 10

IN ACTION

Australia

How many church services have you been to in your life? For me it would be hundreds and not just at one place. Dad was a preacher so we were over the top when it came to going to church, twice on Sundays and then during the week as well. By the time I was a teenager, I'd become an expert at discerning who was the real deal and who wasn't. Some preachers would prattle on forever and never really say anything. Lots of babble of flamboyant words, 'churchy words' that only mean something to a small part of the population. The rest of us would let them float over our heads whilst we drifted off into planning Sunday lunch, or watching the football in the afternoon.

I had a pretty good radar for sweet talkers; those people who would talk the talk but not really walk the walk. Those who'd say all the right kind of things but not really believe it enough to live it out. I guess in a way everyone alive is like this to some extent. What we'd like to be and who we actually were don't always align. However there are some folk in this world that set off big sirens, not quite con-artists, but certainly not genuine. Then others are 100% authentic. I love those in the second category. They say it how it is, no politics, no pretence just straight shooters who make it really clear where they stand. There were enough of these people in my life that made living a life of faith real in the everyday world.

Our building business in Cairns was growing faster than we could manage. There was a boom and Tim was hot property. He would design individual homes for clients and build them at a competitive price undercutting the much bigger firms who had more overheads. At the time of our calling to Malawi, we had 5 houses on the go. Tim had several apprentices, labourers and a team of builders as well as sub-contractors. I was heavily pregnant at this stage so wasn't working full time as a teacher. I would run the office as an administrator from home with Jarred clinging to my legs most of the time.

Typically if you are married to a builder you are either renovating your own house, buying a new one or shifting out of a completed one. This had been my life for the last 10 years. And as Murphy's law goes, whilst about to go into labour with Clayton, we were selling our 'specy' house (display home) that we'd been living in for a year and were moving into a renovator's dream, whist our second 'specy' was being finished off. This new home, had no floor coverings, an entire wall was being smashed out. Dust was everywhere. We had no driveway and no stove. We'd bought it super cheap as a Bank had repossessed it. The owners had missed too many repayments. The owners we figured must have spent too much time in their back shed, which hosted a methamphetamine lab and one-bedroom completely painted black where they obviously had enjoyed themselves. This renovator's dream was a nightmare for this mother who wanted to care for her toddler and was about to bring her new baby into the world. God, what was going on?

I went into labour with Clayton when shopping with Tim's Mum. It is an exciting time when you finally get the green light after nine months of feeling like a beached whale. We'd let the time pass until the contractions were 3 minutes apart and coming strong. By midnight it was time to go to the hospital. I was having what you call a Trial of Scar, meaning that I'd had an emergency cesarean with Jarred but the obstetrician was wanting me to attempt a natural birth. This sounded alright to me at the time. Oh how I wished I'd thought about it now that I know what it means.

Twenty-seven hours of extreme pain, extreme pain with absolutely nothing happening, I was 4 cm dilated when I had arrived in the hospital the day before, and I was still 4 cm. Tim had been on the job site so wasn't really up to speed with all that had happened before we'd gotten to the hospital. He was being supportive, but certainly didn't know anything more than what the midwife was telling us, but I was adamant that something was wrong. I'd pleaded and begged the midwife to get the doctor, I was beside myself from exhaustion and pain. Contractions were back to back and I felt like I was ripping in half, terrified that I'd lose my baby. My sister had lost her first daughter in almost the exact same circumstances, so my fear was real. Tim being torn between my cries for help and a doctor telling him to wait a little longer, didn't quite know what to do. For most of our time we were alone, I was completely naked by now and was in so much pain that I thought my time was up. I was moaning like a dying animal biting down on the nozzle of the gas they'd tried to give me, I prepared myself for the worst. God, why wasn't anyone helping me?

It took a change in shift and a new midwife and doctor to bring my salvation. Finally I was prepared for an emergency caesarian, the baby's heart rate was faint, my blood pressure was through the roof and preeclampsia was threatening to send me into convulsions. I was in shock when some strange man held me still while they did a spinal tap. The wafting of relief surged through my body. By the time I'd caught my breath, I heard the cries of a beautiful baby boy.

Powerlessness is only something you can truly understand when you've experienced it. I was traumatised from Clayton's birth not just emotionally but physically. The uterus wall had been about to rupture, it was worn paper-thin from being in labour too long. The scar that they'd wanted to try was destroyed. An apology from the doctor and a warning about having any more children, was the satisfaction that at least I wasn't crazy.

I knew that something had been wrong and had saved my and my baby's life by fighting for a decision to be made. As a result of the trauma, I had developed pericardial effusion, fluid around my heart. My tiny baby and I were admitted to the coronary care unit. Being separated from Tim, surrounded by those clinging onto life by machines I sat crying out to God cradling my precious child in my arms. Clayton had to breastfeed through the dozens of wires attached to my chest monitoring my every heartbeat. This was not in the happily-ever-after giving birth brochure!

    I was eventually able to go home but was confined to bed rest for the next month. Tim was back on the job but our mothers were in full flight fussing and generally keeping our lives in order. This entire time I couldn't help but wonder, how was I going to survive in Africa? Now talking about trusting God and actioning this took on a whole new meaning. Would I be able to practice what I preached? Could I still believe that God was calling us to serve in Malawi when my own life and that of my children were at stake? Could I jump?

Chapter 11

MAMA MERCY

Malawi

Mama Mercy woke before sunrise every day in her village hut and walked from morning to evening. She carried a big plastic basin on her head calling out "Liponda, Liponda, 3 leaves for 20 kwacha." Meaning "Chinese Cabbage 3 leaves for 5 cents."

It was 7 km from her home to town, she would walk on average 15-20 km a day until her produce was sold. She left early to buy the Chinese cabbage wholesale: 7 leaves for 20 kwacha, so she could make a profit. All this with her 5-month-old baby Anasi on her back. She cried a lot because she was tired and hot and hungry. But Mum was too busy and afraid. Afraid if she stopped she wouldn't have enough money to feed the other children. She had seen hunger too often. She was aware that her pride, her feelings could not get in the way. There was a harshness in her life, her feelings would not get her food, she didn't have the luxury of giving up.

Grandma helped, some days Anasi stayed in the village with her Grandma and other siblings. From 4am to evening she would cry for her mother. She needed to drink, but there was nothing. Grandma would offer her breast for comfort but there was no milk. Mama Mercy came to our ladies group. What were her motives for coming? Perhaps she was only coming to get help? Perhaps she really wanted to hear God's word? She was desperate, and she didn't care what people thought anymore. Whatever the reason for her coming, we loved Mama Mercy. We prayed for her, we cared for her kids, we visited and helped where we could.

We wanted to help Mama Mercy help herself. We hoped to restore her dignity, show love and give her the chance to know her creator. Her body was tired, she struggled with the knowledge that her children were all to different fathers. Men who used her body in return for a small amount of money, perhaps some soap, a new chitenji (sarong). Did she do the right thing? Probably not, but can you blame her? She didn't know that there was a God who intimately cared for her, how amazing that I could sit with Mama Mercy and share with her. She was special, God had a plan and it was good.

Chapter 12

HELPING ROSE

Malawi

Sometimes God has to fit a lot of the puzzle pieces together at one time for us to see what he is doing. This is the way it worked out for our new friend Rose.

Tim, on a day he was usually home, had to go up to the mountain for a meeting. On his way, he saw one of our village leaders riding his bike. It was a chance meeting highlighted by the timing and location; neither were doing what was normal. Baba Issa, the group leader, was miles from home and had been visiting a young girl with a terrible medical problem. Word had spread about the way God had been working answering prayers of the village group. The family had tried all the local options, traditional doctors and the local clinic had failed to help over the years.

Rose had a tumour growing off the side of her neck. It began five years earlier when she had given birth to her child, a physical mark associated with fear, shame and guilt. What had she done to deserve this? Why hadn't the local powers been able to fix it? Baba Issa had been summoned by the family in another attempt to find help and answers.

It was in that moment that Tim happened to pass Baba Issa on the road. Clearly a divine appointment! They shared with the family the love and power of God. His ability to answer prayers in ways we don't understand but need to trust. Were they willing to trust, step out? Were they willing to jump?

Yes, they were. Tim returned home and we shared the story and prayed again, " Lord how do we help this lady? What do we do?" It only took a few hours for our answer to come. That evening we had a visitor, Dr Colin, a South African specialist that lives in Zomba, he loves Jesus and travels to all the government hospitals solving difficult cases. An amazing man who happened to be needing a bed for the night. Not only does Dr Colin help in remote hospitals, he knows the medical system in Malawi. He knew about a European surgeon who worked in Zomba able to help. Puzzle pieces connecting in record time.

Mama Rose, who had never been outside her village, was on her way to the big smoke wide-eyed and full of hope. She returned full of faith. Her face saying a thousand words!! The village chief summoned Baba Issa and Tim. What happened? Explain the faith you are teaching because we want to know.

Chapter 13

INSURANCE

Malawi

We had just got back from our annual leave in South Africa and the 'hungry season' was in full swing. This is a time when the harvest is still about two months away, and the reserves from last year have run low. This year it's particularly tough as many people failed to harvest last season because of widespread national flooding. People were hungry, but it's more than just hunger, people were scared. I had noticed there was an evident fear that came across when we spent time catching up with friends in the local villages we visit regularly.

Today Tim came home with six coconuts, a gift from 'Mama Twaibu'. I guess she and her family were happy to see us, and after the customary catch up she told her son to climb the coconut palm and get us a gift. We used to want to refuse these gifts, thinking how much more these friends needed them than us, but now we usually just say 'thanks', ensuring not to dishonour this gesture. With us accepting it, Mama Twaibu ensured our friendship. She ensured her relationship with an 'asungu' (a foreigner). It ensured her link to someone with 'means', someone who she could call on in times of need. Someone who wouldn't let her or any of her family starve.

As with any relationship, it's complex, and it's dynamic. Last year, at harvest Mama Twaibu gave us a 50kg bag of rice, almost a month's wage. It was very humbling.

INSURANCE

Like a good 'insurance policy', it's wise to have an 'asungu' you can call on, should the need arise. Although some might question the authenticity of this relationship, it's pretty much the 'norm' here in Malawi, and amongst the Yawo. Over the years, we have built trust, respect and honour. She still laughed at my pronunciation of some of their language and still thought 'for a Muslim, I seem to focus a lot on Issa' (Jesus).

Mama Twaibu was just one of the many Yawo people we are seeking to love and share the message of Jesus in a way that will make sense to her, in her language, her culture, sitting under her tree in her village.

Oh, as for the six coconuts, we shared them out with our night guards. I guess if I 'look after' them, then we will sleep well knowing they will in turn 'look after' us!

As we were driving home from Mama Twaibu, I called another friend Saidi, who is a follower of Jesus in a village we visit weekly. I knew he was facing some troubles, so wanted to connect and give some support. Saidi has a great story.

One day he announced after Tim was doing some teaching at his village that he wanted to 'give his life to Jesus', and become one of his followers. Since then, the work of the Spirit has been very evident in his life. It's a different kind of insurance.

The village has elected him as the 'Community Development Co-ordinator'. This basically makes him the 'go-to' guy for any Aid or Development work that happens in the village. He is also one of the Chief's Councilors and recently was appointed a 'Mediator' by the local authority. This has all come about because people know that Saidi is honest and trustworthy. What a great testimony he is!

We'd received a phone call in the middle of the night. It was Saidi calling us to thank us for all that we had done and that he was saying goodbye. Alarmed we asked what was going on. He shared that a delegation of villagers had surrounded his house, all armed with large machetes, threatening to kill him. The Chief had sent them to scare him out of the village. As the story unfolded, I heard him recount that because of the poor harvest last year, his village was selected to be the recipient of 80 bags of maize from one of the many NGO aid and development organisations in Malawi. It was his job to provide a list of 'the most needy' people who would receive the benefit. Now, you can imagine this would always be a tough job, but remember he was elected into the role because of his reputation.

The current village chief put together another list giving it to the Aid organization and claimed it came from Saidi. On this list were only the chief and his immediate family. When all the maize was delivered to the village, only the Chief's family benefited. He'd taken all the maize for himself and his family. Feeling betrayed those missing out turned on the Chief. Then the Chief turned on Saidi. The Chief naturally stated that Saidi was in charge of who received the maize, and in defending himself, Saidi seriously offended the Chief, resulting in the night-time 'hit squad'.

Not so long ago Tim had read to him from Luke 14, the passage titled, 'The cost of being a Disciple'. You know that bit about, 'If anyone comes to me and doesn't hate his father, mother his wife" and "And anyone who does not carry his cross", and "any of you who does not give up everything he has". I have always found this passage tough, and very confronting. It is a cost Saidi knew very well.

The story doesn't end there. After the phone call, Tim and I sat wide awake. What should we do? It was too far away for us to drive there, we'd never make it in time. Instead, we prayed with all our hearts. We claimed the promises of God, we covered Saidi's house with the blood of Jesus. We asked a delegation of angels to guard him. We don't know how long we had been praying for, but the silence was broken by another phone call. "They are gone, I don't know what happened but they just ran away."

We sank to our knees. God is incredible, and his people are covered under his wings. We really don't know what happened that night but we like to picture a giant angel sitting over Saidi's little mud hut. One with a mighty sword that flashes like lightning staring down at those who dared mess with a child of the Most High King. The unseen army sent to defend the humble and righteous.

Chapter 14

COUNTING THE COST

Australia

When we'd had our state and national interviews with our organization and had been accepted as candidates, we were then to go on a journey to raise funds for support and sponsorship to sustain us while we lived in Malawi. This was a time of transition; you pack up your life into a car and spend every second night in a different bed. Tim and I had given ourselves a timeline to finish up the contracts on the homes we'd committed to and then move from Cairns to Brisbane where we were to study for a while, in preparation for service.

It had been a saga bringing Clayton into the world but I'd recovered and our life whilst busy was feeling more normal. The money was pouring in as the work progressed and Tim and I started to wonder about the option of self-funding our time in Malawi. We were certainly on our way and if we gave another few years to our building business we would be able to almost retire. Self- funding this next season would be much easier than having to shake the can and raise support. We'd begun to explore more investment options and asked God to direct us in this. Everything we owned belonged to God and so we were passionate about being good managers of what God had given.

We had three homes close to lock up stage and another nearly finished when cyclone Larry hit. It was a category 5, completely flattening the southern side of Cairns and flooding the rest. We had survived, holding up in our ex-drug dealer's hang out. By then we had a fully functioning kitchen and carpet on the floors. I remember feeding Clayton at night listening to the wail of the wind as it whipped across our roof. The glass doors at the back of the house were flexing in and out and Tim was running around opening and closing windows to depressurize the house. Debris was hitting up against the rock block walls, a tree branch, some corrugated iron, a plastic chair, someone's guttering; the whole house was shaking and it felt like a helicopter was landing on our roof. Jarred slept through the entire thing but Tim, Clayton and I sat in our lounge room watching the show.

We wondered if the houses Tim had left the day before would even be there in the morning. He'd been working 24/7 to get the roofs on, securing the unfinished homes as best as he could before the cyclone hit. Now we just had to wait it out, pray that he'd done enough.

He had! Every one of our houses was still standing. Tim had been careful to abide by the cyclone construction code and the houses were as strong as an ox. They hadn't budged an inch but it wasn't going to be enough to save us. Cyclone Larry brought financial ruin upon us.

Before God, a contract was a contract. We'd promised our clients that we would build them a house for a certain price, and so that is what we did. Prices went through the roof as sub-contractors feasted off the fattened insurance claims. Tilers who only two days ago were charging $20 per square meter were now charging $60 per square meter. The electrician's hourly rate had tripled so had the plasterers, the plumbers and the concreters. We were left standing on the sideline watching the game progress, the money disappeared before our very eyes. Our accountant begged us to reconsider our timeline. With the insurance work bountiful we could make a fortune if we waited another few years, recuperate our losses and end up wealthier than we'd ever been.

In our spirits, we both knew what God was saying to us. This cyclone had been our clear answer. Should we self-fund? No! He wanted to show us that we were to rely completely on him. He wanted to give us our daily bread and not bread enough for the rest of our lives. With heavy hearts, we refused the temptation, finished up our building business and moved to Brisbane. This didn't feel like a brave jump, this felt more like we lost our footing tripped and fell.

Chapter 15
GOD MOMENTS

Malawi

Noticing the God moments in our lives was often the motivation to keep going.

I think I've read somewhere that negative news initiates the most brainwave activity and creates the most impact. Hence, when news is reported in the media it is the negative stuff. We love a good 'terrible story' that shocks. Apparently, it gets our attention better.

I have learnt however, that God likes to work differently to this natural tendency of seeing the cup half empty. He carefully plans each day with moments of blessing and joy that are to be discovered. Like a secret present hidden and waiting.

Recognising this is part of our legacy here in Malawi. If I were to start with the negative each day, I think I would be doing well to get out of bed. There is always way more negative news than I'd like to hear, and it often makes me feel overwhelmed, guilty, useless, like I was emptying the ocean one bucket at a time.

However, God has used our time here to reveal his character of doing the impossible. Nothing is too difficult for Him. He makes a way where there seems to be no way. This is the hope we have. And He cares about the little things. This is what gets me up every morning; the expectation of seeing the impossible.

Faith is believing in what we haven't seen. Trusting in a God of wonders who knows us, every thought we have, every desire even more than we know it ourselves. We try to spend our dinner times, as a family, sharing stories of these God moments, a bit like sharing the 'highs and lows' of the day. We have stories of amazing healings, people coming to faith, favour being shown in Government Offices, conflicts resolved, marriages reunited, friends made and even electricity staying on for one more hour so I could finish the budget that was due.

My favourites were the stories that show unbelievable generosity. Answers to prayers that really didn't need to happen, God not only supplied our needs but also catered to our wants, just because he could. Clayton announced one day that he wanted a cat. He loved animals and already had many pets, however a cat he had not.

One day we all had a bit of a laugh. We're not really a cat kind of family, Tim most of all. He called them the 'spawn of satan' (sorry cat lovers, there's not a lot of love there.) He's allergic to them for a start and doesn't like them because he said they see the world from above and everyone else is under them. People were there to serve. You couldn't train them to obey like a dog, they pee everywhere. In a group of people, they'd always choose to sit on the lap of the person who doesn't like them the most. You get the picture.

So that night Clayton started to pray for a cat. (I think that night Tim prayed that Clayton didn't get a cat.) Would you believe what happened?

A month or so later, the boys ran into the house holding the smallest kitten you have ever seen. God had answered Clayton's prayers. A kitten, born under a building in our compound. Just one, barely able to walk, eyes just opened, poor abandoned little kitten that needed to be loved. "Can we keep him?"

It's funny how God answers the prayers of a child. The cat had to live outside and could only come into the schoolroom. He was beautiful, even for me, who's afraid of the randomness of cats. He would snuggle on my lap and go to sleep, drink milk out of a dropper and wait patiently every day for us to come to get him. Don't worry, Tim grew to like the cat, God had answered his prayers too. No sneezing, it saw Tim as the boss, it peed outside and it never sat on his lap! God just loves to spoil us but he never wants us to act spoilt.

Tim got his spoiling, not long after that when we prayed for a boat motor. He had built a boat made out of local timber so that our family could enjoy Lake Malawi. It lasted a while but disintegrated. So we had to pray for a boat. It didn't take very long before we found an old one at ex-pat friend's, cousin's brother's place 100kilometres north sitting under an old tarp for 10 years. Tim has become quite good at fibreglassing and boat repairs. He even knows which company in South Africa that sells the right kind of fibreglass who can connect with a local guy with a transport business. (Now that is another story.)

We needed a motor for this 'new' 50-year-old boat, so we prayed for one. One day Tim spied it while shopping for car parts in Lilongwe, the capital city. It was owned by an Indian guy who didn't really know what it was. It sat at the back of the shop and had been there for over 5 years. He saw it, took some photos and then went back home to Mr Google. It seemed a decent brand and it wasn't all that old.

With a coke bottle of fuel in hand and a bucket of water and a connection to our car battery, Tim and the Indian businessman tried out the motor. It burst into life and sat there idling away. 'How much do you want for it?" Knowing it was worth thousands. "A couple of hundred dollars." Thank you, Jesus!

So we now use our recreation time cruising on Lake Malawi with our fibreglass boat and it's 40 hp motor!

Oh and to top it all off, this year for Jarred's birthday, Tim found a waterski hidden in a shop at the markets! A bit of rope and a bamboo handle. Voila! The Downes' are water skiing on Lake Malawi!!! (Yes it's tricky and takes a while to get up.)

God of wonders spoiling us, we just need the faith to ask.

Chapter 16

EASY MONEY

Malawi

"Mama I'm hungry". This is not an unusual request but coming from Hanifu, it was. He was a good kid, well-spoken with beautiful deep village Ciyawo. He was an extremely respectful and very talented boy. Jarred and Clayton took to him straight away. He'd moved in across the road; the one-bedroom shack that is known for its high turnover in tenants. People who have nowhere else to go, end up there. It's cheap and separate from the village. It has no water, no cooking facilities and sits in the blazing sun. Those who come never stay long.

I went with Hanifu to meet his mother, a beautifully dressed Yawo lady who greeted me with a sparkle in her eyes. She didn't look like a 'Wakulaga' (one who was suffering). I introduced myself and met her older daughter and her newborn child. She showed me into the hut, it was immaculate. Clean and tidy, well organized and set out. What was her story?

Her husband worked with the government but had left her and gone to South Africa, the land of milk and honey. I've heard this story a hundred times. Men leave their entire families going after the dream of wealth in the promised land. This story had me vexed, why leave when you already have a job? The stories about South Africa were getting bigger and better by the year. He finally couldn't resist. Hanifu's mother had tried her best to make do with the money she had left. But now it was all gone. They had no food. I made arrangements for her to start a small business and gave her enough food to last a little while. She wanted me to pray with her and ask God for wisdom.

Hanifu came to play every day, it was a joy to see them bounce back in his step. He listened to every word we taught at the kids' group and loved helping around the house. One early evening Hanifu was in the car with Tim when they saw his sister ahead in the street. Hanifu averted his eyes and pretended he didn't see her. Surprised Tim commented and was taken back by Hanifu's simple and heavy answer, "She's getting us money," she was surrounded by a few young men who were requesting her 'services', a quick way to make money. Hanifu added, "Mum knows about it, but what can she say? My sister is making more money than Mum ever could."

I would love to say Tim and I have never heard of such a thing before but we have way too many times. I'd like to stand on moral ground and condemn such behaviour, but if I was left in such circumstances, would I be any different? This is now very commonplace behaviour in our region. The mixture of traditional Yawo culture and the western influence is resulting in a casserole of controversy. We struggle with the tension and pray God will make the way for families like Hanifu's.

Chapter 17

THE FIRST CROCODILE STORY

Malawi

Those of us who have lived in Far North Queensland are accustomed to the odd 'Danger Crocodile' sign at rivers, beaches and creeks. Some of us who are rather lax, even ignore these signs in some of the most popular swimming holes, as we have swum there forever and have never seen a croc. It seems the Australian Government has decided that if there is a sign on every watercourse then they are legally covered for negligence. Consequently, it is almost impossible to find any decent swimming hole, outside backyard pools, that doesn't have a croc warning sign nearby.

This, of course, is the complete opposite to our reality here in Malawi. Would you believe I have never seen a crocodile warning sign here? Apart from actually seeing the crocodile itself sunning on the bank, there is nothing to indicate danger. We can even get a false sense of security from all the local folk swimming and washing in the river and lake.

It has always been said that the river is loaded with crocs and hippos but not the lake so much. I don't know if that was just to make everyone feel better or there actually was an imaginary boundary where the river flows out into the lake. Either way, we would carefully motor our boat down the river avoiding the pods of hippo and watching the eyes watching us. Then we would all sigh a breath of relief when the river opened out to the lake.

Of course, the local guys fishing in their little dugout canoes assured us that there were no crocs in the lake, especially where we were swimming. Strength in numbers can also help the facade, making sure we were swimming in an area where there were other people. The lake where we swim always has ladies washing from sun up to sundown. We had never seen a crocodile there, and had spent hours swimming and boating in this area.

Well, that was until the other day. There is a crocodile farm (yes believe it or not) up the road. I am assuming it originally was an ex-pat innovation as most things like that are. We had been there several times with the kids. It isn't exactly like Australia Zoo but you could hold the little crocs and collect teeth that were lying around. There were hundreds of crocodiles there ranging from newborns to the massive five-meter ones, held in a tiny pen protected by chicken wire.

Rumour has it that a government official had heard about the place and threatened an inspection. Now as Malawi goes this generally relates to money, not sincere concern and welfare for the poor, dear animals. The Croc farm owner got edgy about the kwacha (dollars) involved and so decided the best plan to avoid the issue was to release the crocs into the lake. Apparently, 150 were released to roam freely in beautiful Lake Malawi! The impact of this has been playing out over the last few years and the results are devastating.

With a massive over population and not enough food to go around, many of these crocs have become pests in populated areas. Goats and cows are frequently taken. I had recently heard of a tug of war between a crowd of people holding the legs of a cow and a huge crocodile holding the neck. The croc was defeated in the end and swam away to leave the cow as the real loser. With the people quickly gathering to slit its throat under Islamic prayers ensuring the meat at least could be eaten.

Although these stories have been buzzing around in conversation through the village grapevines, there was a much deeper meaning behind it all. You see, crocodiles have a deep spiritual connection in the world of Traditional African Religion. They are like snakes, a clear form of evil. Some say they are witch doctors that have transformed themselves and are serving to make restitution for curses and black magic. Others believe they are a form of Satan himself roaming to destroy those who have not protected themselves. The increase in population was attributed to an increase in spiritual power in the area, with many villagers becoming more afraid of them and the attacks that were happening more and more frequently. Locals would never kill a croc or eat its meat in fear of the spiritual repercussions.

In contrast, enter my husband, the 'Croc Hunter Extraordinaire'. After hearing of six deaths from croc attacks in the last month, my husband A.K.A the croc hunter decided to go and 'fix' the situation. He and a mate got together a crossbow attached to a fishing line and ventured out in the dead of night in our boat. They quickly found dozens of beady eyes all following their every move. The air was tense, the night thick and the water was oily black, swirling slowly around them.

In the midst of all this, Jarred, Clayton and I were back at Tim's mate's house with his wife and daughter. While they were out in the darkness, the rest of us were all rather jovial about their croc hunting quest and were having a few laughs at the expense of them being 'croc heroes'.

They were surrounded by the enemy. They had shut down the motor and were silently rowing themselves through the blanket of weeds. Their hearts were racing and fear was filling the night. Tim's years of kangaroo and rabbit shooting in the Territory as a boy, had all come into play. A shot was made, a shadow leapt out of the water nearly tipping the boat. The fishing line peeled off, snapping the line like a piece of cotton. The race was on the hunters against the hunted.

(In the middle of all this, I decided to give them a call to see how it was all going.) The entire dramatic atmosphere was ruined by a noise piercing the night.

"Tim your wife is calling you!"

Frustrated by the lack of respect towards the battle of man against beast, the phone was answered.

" Hi, how's it all going? (giggle, giggle) Have you got anything yet? (open belly laugh)"

"What? Don't ring us now!"

"Those girls have no respect!"

Without knowing what they'd hit they ventured deeper into the marsh. The boat was compromised in the shallow water. Where these ancient reptiles lurked. "There's only one thing to do, mate. Kaboom! What happened next? No one shall ever know! I couldn't say for sure but wouldn't it be nice to know that there were two fewer crocodiles to terrorize the villages?

Despite this audacious quest, it was decided that perhaps this wasn't the safest way to confront the problem. Tim tracked down a "Malawian parks and wildlife ranger". I put this in quotations because he was really a local guy whose job is to shoot crocs. We told him about all the attacks in the area, about the village people's terror to go to the lake or wash in the river. How people were risking their lives to get the water they desperately needed to live. How the lake and river are the lifeblood for the people. Not a word made a difference, but a bit of encouragement of another kind got our local hunter to make an appearance. He totaled 22 crocs just in the section of river closest to town, a decent effort but only really scratching the surface of the problem.

Fortunately for us, we live about 2km from the river, so at least we are safe enough in our beds at night from croc attacks. However, we do leave the compound. On a walk with my friend down near the swamp, a crowd running the other way enveloped us. Two crocs were crossing the road in front of us. Not an everyday occurrence for me but enough to make me take another route.

Chapter 18

THE SECOND CROCODILE STORY

Malawi

It is strange how there is a love, hate relationship with these ancient creatures. The danger associated with them draws some in like a romantic love song. For others, there is a clear fear that commands obedience. It seems in our family, we have those on both sides of the fence.

Tim recently went to Lilongwe, the capital city to meet up with one of our Global Consultants. When travelling on the roads in Malawi, it is rather different from the Western world. Pedestrians use the roads as much as vehicles. It could be described more like an aisle in a shopping centre than a road, with stalls lining both sides and an unlimited amount of goods of all varieties being sold. Goods ranging from the lining of a car tire used as rope, (This stuff holds Africa together.) to chickens, fruit and vegetables, goats, furniture, mats, cooking pots and material.

On his journey to Lilongwe, you wouldn't believe what Tim happened to come across? Yes, you are right. It was all rather secretive and exciting, so Tim made arrangements. The story came home and our kids nearly jumped out of their skins. They were going to be heroes. My warning fell on deaf ears, " If you must, please get the smallest, least dangerous, just out of the egg kind."

Now small is a relative term. This thing they bought home didn't fit my definition. Just under a metre. (Well at least it wasn't 5 metres long!) It had a rubber band holding its jaws and was put in our backyard sandpit. Our boys were wearing welding gloves practicing picking it up by the back of the neck so it couldn't turn and bite their fingers off. Tim was standing nearby explaining the basic dos and don'ts. (I'm not quite sure where he obtained his expertise.) I entered this scene with our loyal Gardener, Baba Donard. "Mama you aren't going to like this", he said. And he was right.

Normally I am not one to frighten easily, I have held all sorts of creatures at zoos and nature parks, including crocs. I have allowed my family lots of rope in their adventures, but this time was different. I felt a cold chill enter me as soon as I saw it. It was like its beady eyes were looking into my soul. It slowly dragged its tail toward our youngest son, and panic hit me.

I was going to vomit, I was going to faint. That thing was wrong in every sense and I couldn't allow it in our family. Being the good Yawo women that I am, I just walked away quietly leaving the rest of our workers with Tim and the boys. Inside our home I flopped onto our bed, "God what am I going to do. Please help me. I hate that thing, I want it out."

Soon our youngest, who has always been sensitive, came looking for me.

"Mum, don't you like our new pet?"

"No, Clayton I don't."

"Why?"

"It is too dangerous."

"But Daddy says it is alright, as long as we are careful."

What to say? What to do? Tim and I always backed each other, and yet here I was clearly standing on the other side of the fence. Clayton left, but returned with Jarred and Tim, both glowing with excitement over the new adventure.

"How cool is our croc Mum?" said Jarred before he saw the look on my face. "What's wrong?"

"Dad, Mum doesn't like our new pet."

"What?" Tim entered the room. "Really? You don't normally mind?"

Well, yes all that was true. I began to explain how I felt the evil of the thing, how it was like a snake and that all it could do was to bring danger into our family. My sensitivity to the spiritual connotations of the thing was off the scale. I was peaking with an awareness of the potential danger looming. I guess this could be attributed to a mother's instinct or merely a protective survival response to danger. There was no way that I could allow this thing to stay.

At the look on my face, Jarred began to tear up. Tim realized that I was seriously affected and a family meeting was held. Later that night, our new pet was disposed of. A sense of relief flowed like a river. "Thank you, sweet Jesus!" But the story does not finish there.

Two days later, a report came from friends who live next to the river. A teenage boy was taken, whilst he stood in ankle-deep water washing his feet. Those around him were so scared of the spiritual power, they didn't say a word as they saw the crocodile creep up onto the bank. As the boy yelled for help, the bystanders ran the other way. The fear of being punished for interfering was greater. The crocs were getting so confident now that they are attacking right up on the riverbank.

The next day as I passed by some local men I knew, I heard them speaking of the attack. They both knew about our pet incident and were discussing the issue.

"Mama you were right to fear that evil in your house."

"Thank you, you know Baba Tim does care about me a lot, so he got rid of it"

"Yes, he did what was right to care for his family."

A few hours later, Tim met one of the men still discussing the same topic.

"Baba Tim, you know that because we took one of their young, they have taken one of ours."

"What?" Silence. "We'd better pray about this, and ask God for protection"

"Yes thank you, Baba."

Tim was not being blamed for the incident, but the deep connections between the natural world and the spiritual realm cannot be dismissed in this community. Our natural instincts don't always give us the answers we need. Our scientific understanding can only go so far and our worldview isn't necessarily accurate. But by the grace of God do we stand, and stand we shall as long as we hold tight and listen to him.

You see, we all make crazy decisions at times, and it is possible for us all to get it wrong. The biggest mistakes we can make in life are often not a result of ignorance. I think our biggest blunders come from our own pride, the arrogance of our own knowledge. Possibly the greatest danger comes not from what we don't know, but instead from what we think we do know. Confidence in ourselves and our thinking drives us to believe in a world of our own making.

The longer we are here, the more I question my own understanding.

Proverbs 3:5-6 says it well, *"Trust in the Lord with all your heart and lean not on your own understanding. In all your ways acknowledge him and he will make your paths straight."*

Chapter 19

NOT MY SON

Australia

Up until I became a mother myself, I had no idea what it was really like to love your child. The instincts that kick in are primal and so strong that it is almost scary. As soon as my boys were born I knew without a doubt I'd protect them with my life. Heaven help anyone who would get in my way. I think God does this on purpose because these tiny lives completely destroy any sense of normal you thought you once had. Jarred was a hard adjustment but Clayton tipped me over the edge of sanity. (Sorry darling, Mummy still loves you!)

As it turned out, Clayton was born with a food protein intolerance to dairy, soy and wheat. That was so easy to write, yet defined my world for 2 ½ years. He was only a month old when we noticed him beginning to break out in a rash. It started small so I didn't worry too much (I'm not a panicky mother), but it got worse. The doctor said it was eczema and gave us some cream to try. (I can hear all you mothers of allergic children groan from here!) The cream didn't work and Clayton got a whole lot worse.

There was a pattern emerging, he'd feed really well (I was breastfeeding at the stage) then he'd begin to get whiney. The cry would become a scream and then he'd become hysterical and inconsolable. This would go on for hours with Tim and I not knowing what to do. We'd go to the emergency at the hospital to be told that there is nothing wrong with our child.

Clayton became completely covered in eczema so much so that he bled in all the cracks in his skin, he looked like he was falling apart. The layer of skin on his bottom would turn into red welts, blister and then peel until the entire layer of skin was gone and a weeping mess left behind. Tim and I resorted to literally mummifying him each day by dipping clean chux cloths in olive oil and covering his entire body then sedating him in an attempt to give him respite. We went to eleven doctors and specialists in the hope of finding an answer. Deliriously tired, beside ourselves, we moved house to Brisbane in preparation of service in Africa! Praise the Lord! (I'm being sarcastic!)

Years ago if I'd ever heard of parents abusing their children, I'd be horrified, and completely disgusted at this unacceptable behaviour. Not that I condone any form of abuse, but since having Clayton, I now know that if you are sleep deprived, starving yourself because everything you seem to eat makes your baby sick, your husband is working 15 hour days and every doctor you go to cannot help, it is very easy to be tempted to try anything to get some peace.

Desperate to get away from his uncontrollable screaming, I remember one day wrapping up Clayton, putting him in his cot, giving his medicine to sedate him and then going outside to the end of our driveway and bursting into tears. It was one of the lowest points in my life. I was broken; I couldn't do it anymore. God if you are going to take my baby, please do it now, I give him to you. I lay there in the gutter, blocking out Clayton's cries, 2-year-old Jarred playing with his truck around me. I don't know how long I was there, but I do remember that nothing happened. No answer came, no voice from heaven, no angel of light; just Jarred and his truck and a screaming Clayton waiting for me.

A mother's instincts should be listened to even if she is the only one in the world saying it. I'd known this was not a behavioural issue that some doctors suggested, I'd known that this had much more to do with his stomach and digestion and not the eczema that I had been given dozens of creams for. I was trialing every combination of food I could get my hands on to see if it was giving him the allergic reaction. I just couldn't seem to get a break, everyway I turned didn't seem to offer any solution. There was nothing I could do but keep on keeping on. Days rolled into weeks and weeks into months. By the time Clayton was 10 months old, we were able to get a government subsidised specialist infant formula called Neocate. We had to knock on a lot of doors and tick a lot of boxes to get approval. It is the last resort for babies with feeding issues. This was at least something different to try, maybe it was the cure we'd been praying for?

Unfortunately, this answer didn't come with a silver lining, Clayton hated it, I didn't blame him it was horrible. To get him on it, we had to starve him until he was so hungry and thirsty that he would drink. Doesn't this sound like such a lovely family activity? Not! What mother wants to take such drastic measures? By now we were in Brisbane and the 6 months waiting list for the Pediatric Gastroenterologist had found us.

At 18 months Clayton was diagnosed with a food protein intolerance to dairy, soy and wheat. This was the first time a doctor had been able to give Clayton's condition a name. He went on to describe all the symptoms Clayton had been experiencing. He explained that those who suffer are in excruciating pain as the absorption filaments in the bowel are ripped off by the digestion process. Tim and I sat there completely silenced. Our baby had been beside himself in pain for his entire life and this was the first person who had the expertise to help us. We held Clayton close and sobbed and sobbed.

It was then that I decided I didn't want to jump anymore, I didn't want to take my baby to Africa! God what you are asking me to do it's too hard, I can't do it.

Chapter 20

WAIT

Malawi

Mama Shakila sat under the little covered area she had made out of bamboo. She has been there since sunrise and she would stay until evening. She felt blessed that she had a garden, the soil was close to the river, it was fertile and well-watered. She only had to dig a meter or so to find the water table. Her watering can was heavy but the tomatoes were growing well. She had already begun selling the Chinese cabbage. Seeing the money come in makes her heart swell. She was doing it, making her way in life.

Mama Shakila has five children. She was still breastfeeding the youngest one but the others were at school. She wanted what is best for them and so she would work to make it happen. Suddenly she jumped up waving her arms and shouting, rocks flying and goats scattering everywhere, far enough away to miss the rocks but not far enough to miss out on Mama Shakila's tomatoes.

The goats would remain in battle with her the entire day, then come back tomorrow for more. The hippos would come at night. Could she beat them? I didn't know, but we sat together and prayed. We prayed over the field, we prayed for her kids, for her husband for their future. That they wouldn't be hungry this year.

Mama Shakila has a history of trusting God and she wouldn't stop now. I would continue to help her, I gave her some bamboo from our garden to make a fence, I bought some of her produce, I would love her and I would help her help herself. Mama Shakila didn't need my charity, she needed my friendship, we learnt from each other and we journeyed together in our faith. As I sat and looked out over the gardens, I saw a dozen other women in the same situation. I worried about them. I worried about them differently. Did they have the faith of Mama Shakila? Did they have the security she did? We prayed for them and waited on God for his answers.

Chapter 21

IDA

Malawi

Often those who are on the supporting end of missionary service don't get to see or experience the impact of their prayers.

"God Bless the Missionaries" prayers are often uttered but what impact does that really have?

Well, let me tell you what happens when people in sending countries find time in their day to sit and pray for those they have sent into the mission field.

We were heading out to dinner as a team. It had been a hard week full of people, problems, poverty, begging and sickness. The levels of our emotional energy were depleted as we gave of ourselves again and again. Compassion Fatigue is very common on the field and we were experiencing the effects of what happens when you give of yourself, addressing problems that won't be solved in our lifetime.

We decided a trip to a local restaurant together would be fun and take our minds off the difficulties around us. Two cars, we were second. Tim drove with our family in the car plus, Liz our team member. We decided that Garth Brooks was a good option for the evening so were having fun singing together. (Sorry to admit we weren't being all that spiritual. However, it is a good reality check to advise you that Missionaries do do things other than just read the Bible and pray.)

We were travelling the Lake Road that is one of the bigger roads in the area. The road was well travelled by many heading through to the lake, the capital city or Mozambique. Dodging goats, bikes, chickens and people was very common. Tim was well experienced in navigating these obstacles.

Suddenly out of the crowd on the side of the road ran a little girl named Ida; a moment of horror when she appeared in our headlights. There was nothing we could do. I still hear that horrible thud that echoed through my body. We had been going the speed limit 100km. There wasn't a chance of stopping in time. Tim hit the brakes, slowing the car without rolling us. He managed to dodge the people on both sides of the road.

The car was surrounded by people screaming. We were screaming and crying, and praying. "Please Lord let her not be dead." In a matter of seconds, the little girl was scooped up and put in my arms, blood all over her, her body limp. Her mother, a screaming mess on the road, was pushed into our car. Tim yelled some instructions to those standing nearby and we drove off to the hospital.

At this moment we witnessed eight miracles in succession.
1. We were not mobbed by the angry bystanders. God had kept enough peace for us to keep our heads, act quickly and get out of there. (Malawian travel advice says never to stop, as lynching is very common.)
2. As we travelled we prayed aloud. "Lord let her live, let her live". She woke up. She was not dead!
3. As I checked over her body, I found the source of her blood. She was only cut on the leg!
4. We got to the hospital and went straight through to emergency. There were doctors on duty able to help us. (Although they didn't really clean the wound, nor did they have any medicine.)
5. The family was Yawo, meaning we could speak to them. The little girl was talking to me telling me where she hurt.
6. The cut in her leg only needed stitches. There was no ligament or tendon damage!

7. We saw the mark of her eyebrow on the wheel arch of our car. The burnt hair contrasting to the white paint. The only thing on the car made of plastic. It had given a bit when she was hit. Tim had managed to miss hitting her straight on. The bull bar on our Hilux would have killed her for sure. Instead, she had bounced off the side of the car, her leg flicking up hitting the side rail.
8. As we took little Ida and her mother back to the village we met the family wailing as if it was a funeral, her funeral. We were able to settle them down and show them, Ida. The whole family began praising God.

We spent the next week or so taking Ida and her mother back to the local clinic to get treatment. There is a whole other story involved in getting decent treatment here but let's focus on the positive. We were able to find enough medication to stop the infection.

Ida is now home with her family running around, staying very far away from the busy road!

We are so very thankful for God's mercy. We never did get out to dinner. But I guess we were restored in another way. But by the grace of God do we stand. We will probably never know who was praying for us at that time. But we are convinced that it's often the prayer of others that support and carry us in times of extreme stress. Please know that even the most simple of prayers can move mountains, or in this case, save the life of a little girl!

Chapter 22

POWER PLAY

Malawi

I am one of those people who can wake in the morning and remember what I dreamt about. This is normally a good thing unless it is a disturbing dream. One night I had one of those disturbing dreams. So real that I thought I was awake until I actually woke up and wondered where I was. I told the dream to Tim and we prayed.

We had experienced in the past that such dreams can be connected to things happening in the Spirit world. It is always good to cover ourselves in prayer. (This might be a stretch for those not having lived in Animist cultures.)

The following day I went to the village with Tim to minister to the groups. Our time was rich with prayer and explaining God's word. On the way home, one group member whom I know well asked us to escort her to the place where her sick daughter was staying. She was with the 'sing'anga', a traditional healer who uses a combination of natural medicine and spiritual rituals and charms.

I sat in the little hut, very aware that the Spirit I came with was not the same spirit that the 'sing'anga' was using. To my surprise, the traditional African healer was a woman. We sat and chatted about the sickness, when it began and what was wrong. They had already been to the local hospital and got medicines that didn't work. The traditional healer was fighting spirits, bad spirits that were creating this sickness.

It is well known here that there are types of African sicknesses that cannot be healed by western medicines. I explained that my faith was in the power of God through our mediator Jesus. That there was only one God and he was the giver and taker of life. Through his power only can a person be truly healed, he was the creator of all spirits and at his command, they must submit to him. This sing'anga was fascinated, we spoke for a long time and she wanted this power but wasn't prepared to make any personal submission to Jesus as the saviour to get it.

We laid hands on and prayed over the girl. The African healer sat next to me and acknowledged that there was a particular power in my prayer. Power encounters are common here, my dream had been a warning for what I was to face that day. I am very thankful that God keeps us covered in the battle, without him, I am powerless and have nothing to offer.

Chapter 23

SING IT

Malawi

Ever tried to memorize a long passage? Perhaps studying for an exam or learning a bible passage? It's hard. Well, we decided to teach the beatitudes from Matthew 5 for our kids' club. We had over 100 kids coming those days. Parents willing to trust us to teach their children the right thing, a mix of Christian and Muslim kids all learning together, rather an odd situation really.

Blessed are the poor in spirit for theirs is the kingdom of heaven, blessed are they that mourn; for they shall be comforted. There is a lot to learn both in the words themselves and the meaning they give.

'You know, we are the Yawo, the poorest of the poor, who know what it is like to suffer.' A new believer was telling Tim. 'You only need God when you are suffering, it makes you stay close to him.' A sobering shiver went through me as I realized how true this was.

These kids needed to know this, the truth that would give them hope through the hard times. We'd spent seven weeks going through the verses, repeating them again and again. The kids were putting me to shame, working hard to please, they could recite what they were hearing, but how could they remember it for the future?

Singing! In the traditional initiation ceremonies over 300 songs can be used. If we sing our brains somehow remember the words. I can indeed drag up songs from early preschool years, that I hadn't heard for decades. So sing it we did. 'Upile, upile, Mlungu wape upile' Blessings, blessings God will give blessings. You can hear it chanted over and over again. It worked so well that on the day we finished teaching, even the 3-year-olds could sing the song and do the actions on their own.

By the end, I wasn't really sure who was teaching who. So humbling is it to be in the presence of a child's innocent faith.

Chapter 24

THE BLACK ROOM

Malawi

The room was black. The only light crept through the gaps in the blocked up window. The air was thick and the smell was overpowering. I could hear my friend's daughter groaning. We had just finished our village meeting under the mango tree. It has been a time of truth and openness. We talked about what God was doing in our lives and how can we take his word and apply it.

Tim and Baba Windi and Baba Saidi were asking for prayer when my friend solemnly announced that her daughter might die soon. This is the same one I had prayed for in the traditional healer's hut the week before. The traditional medicines hadn't brought any change. Without really knowing what medicines or practices were actually done, it was hard to determine whether any good came from them. Sometimes they are just simple, like a tree bark soaked in water to be drunk, other times they are a mixture of all sorts of strange ingredients; hair, roots, blood, sap, teeth that are ground up boiled and inserted into the body via cuts or even blown into the anus.

My friend's daughter was lying on a bed made of plaited pandanus palms on a crude bed frame of bound logs. The mud hut was like an oven, the tin roof creaking in the heat. She was crying and moaning while her mother sat sadly quiet in the corner. We had decided that the whole village group was going to pray for her this time. She wasn't really aware of us, but some of the ladies gathered her into a sitting position.

Stomach cancer was what the hospital had said many months ago, they'd sent her home with only a few tablets. There was really nothing else they could do when palliative care is non-existent. We gathered around her placing our hands on her thin body. With a cacophony of words floating in the room, we asked God to come upon this woman and give her peace. We rebuked the sickness and told it to leave in the name of Jesus Christ. We declared the promises of God's word over her and we sang softly bringing glory to God. A strong sense of unity enveloped us, and our sick friend quieted down, then slept.

A silent strength drew us together as we gathered outside. Each woman offered time to sit by and pray over her so she wouldn't be left alone. She needed our prayers to bring her peace. We were to stand in the gap as the fight for her life rolled on. Tim, Baba Windi and I were quiet in our thoughts dictated by the heaviness of our hearts. This is not the first time we have done such things and the spirit realm was tangible. We were all still speaking to the Lord about this in our hearts. Was he going to heal her this time?

A week later, Tim and Windi returned to the group. Before the teaching began a very happy mother bounced into the group. "Baba come and see, come and see."

They followed her to the same hut with the same girl. Rounding the corner, they saw two people sitting on a mat eating ugali. It was her, a broad smile appeared on her face. She'd been released from the battle, God had bought her some time!

Chapter 25

IT WAS JUST A RIOT!

Malawi

Malawi has so many adventures to offer those willing to take a risk. This particular day on the menu was a local riot, between the Islamic community and the Christian one.

Now it was time for more prayer as it all breaks out. Just another drama to add to the pile!! Liz (our teammate) and I were laughing. This was crazy. We thought we had covered most dramas by now in our adventure of sharing the gospel with the Yawo, but we were proved wrong. Riots weren't part of that list! Medevac's, car accidents, epidemics, no food, no fuel, no water, no electricity, death threats, armed robberies and now a riot!! And yet we were laughing about it. Either we had just gone completely mad or God's grace was sufficient!

I had just talked to Keith today, a friend and fellow missionary living an hour away, about his own drama. The fuel station had accidentally filled his car with petrol instead of diesel. Glad to hear it was finally sorted, (no roadside assistance here) we felt like we were playing poker. Does a car breaking down beat a riot? Does a flush beat a straight? What sort of game were we playing? Our lives were never boring.

The story on the grapevine was that someone had been caught selling pork in the market. The Islamic community was furious. No one would ever dare to do such a thing. This act of ignorance or defiance opened a massive can of worms.

We have a community of Apostolics squatting in the nearby forest. They all wear white robes just like Jesus and live by a certain radical code. Some Islamic troublemakers in their anger went there and began to burn down and loot their makeshift grass houses. I don't really know how this was related to the selling of pork. The police were called. The situation got out of hand and tear gas was used to settle the crowds. More and more people joined the riot and the police could do nothing. In an act of rage or stupidity, two teenage boys attacked the police and were shot as a result.

The protesting Islamic community got word of this and began to go crazy. We have a few small convenience stores here. They were trashed by the angry mob, particularly the stores selling alcohol. The entire market was shut down, and police were facing the riot with tear gas and live shots into the crowd. From the safety of my house, I could hear the crowd of people chanting and the sound of police sirens. Our compound about 500 metres away from all the action.

There was a sense of peace as we waited it out. I am amazed that God is never surprised at these things. So often what was meant for harm is used for good. So we waited with anticipation. What would come from all this? Would it help the work of reaching the Yawo or make it harder? Only time would tell, and with God, you just never know his timing.

It is always an irony that such things happen when Tim is away. The boys and Tim were in Blantyre, a major city 3 hours drive away, taking Ben, our temporary admin guy to the airport. He had finished his time with us and was flying back to Australia. Poor guy missing out on all the fun!

Tim half-jokingly had shown me the paintball gun before he left. After a recent armed robbery, we got it as a means of defense. You can swap the soft balls for hard ones that won't kill a person but will certainly stop them in their tracks. I scoffed at him earlier that morning, "As if I am going to need that!" Well with the police using tear gas, and real guns, they will hardly call on me with my paintballs! Tim called to check I was alright as our friend the local police inspector had rung instructing us all to remain in 'lockdown' mode for the rest of the day. I could smell the tear gas as it wafted in the breeze.

Liz was at her house in the other compound across the road. We were the only ex-pats on site. When we are in 'lockdown mode' we don't leave the house and no one comes in or out of the compound. Exciting stuff? Well not really. I was in the middle of the village Adult Literacy Exams. We had to cancel the groups for the day.

So inside we stayed. Calling each other now and again to check all is well. I was getting lots of paperwork done, all those reports that should have been done but I never found the time to do. Tim kept calling me regularly as the police were giving him updates. They had offered to come to our compound and provide extra protection. I managed to wake up our Ministry Director in Head Office, Australia in the middle of the night to advise him of the situation. Liz and I had packed our bags just in case we needed to make a run for it.

Our ever-faithful 70-year-old gardener, Baba Jenson, sat near the front gate all day, punga knife in hand diligently guarding me. He was so protective, especially when Tim was away. Our friends Baba Akim and Baba Bilali went down to the market. They said the man selling the pork had been arrested. There would be a court hearing. Keeping the guy locked up was probably the best way for him to stay alive. There was lots of tension around. I had heard there was an increased police presence patrolling, more police from Zomba, a town two hours away, had arrived and began to disperse the crowd. A massive storm had been brewing all afternoon. What the police failed to do in calming the crowd, God sorted, with a giant crack of thunder and downpour. I love God's sense of humour.

Clearly, this is a place that needs to hear about the saving grace of God. If such things weren't happening, we could all pack up and go home. It is good confirmation that the battle is raging and we are in a war. It's a spiritual war that sometimes manifests itself physically. It is important not to lose sight of the big picture. We shouldn't be surprised if we hear about wars and rumours of wars. We live in a broken world.

I have to be careful not to become too blasé about such things. I had adrenaline pumping for a while, but as is the case in such situations, better to hide and to just wait it out, rather than risk unnecessary danger. Sitting in the corner quaking with fear isn't very practical, so in good Aussie style, we found the funny side of the whole thing. In our hiding, Liz and I spent the afternoon thinking of inappropriate comments and courageous feats of heroism. Of course, we were all talk, making the most of a terrible situation. We thought we were hilarious. When all of this was over; I had another traumatic experience to talk to the counselor about one day. Thank you for praying for our safety. There were later several other major political riots some of which we had to evacuate. Praise God that he always kept us safe.

Chapter 26

TRUST AND BLAME GAMES

Malawi

In the NGO world, and in 'Development Theory', trust, or more importantly the 'lack of trust', is one of the major contributing factors leading to the depth of poverty many countries like Malawi experience. People can turn on each other in a heartbeat if it means getting ahead. It's a deep-rooted survival mentality, a system, a way of thinking. Those who don't play this game, don't last long, there is no backup plan, there is no social service, you do what you can or you won't survive.

After returning from a week away in Mozambique, Tim was met by a delegation of our compound staff wanting to report the incident of a missing duck, our duck. It hadn't been seen since we left for the Conference, and its disappearance was a mystery. A thorough search had been carried out by our workers but to no avail. It was expected that Tim 'the boss', make a ruling in this case of 'the missing duck,' or the 'duck gate' scandal! It's difficult to portray the seriousness of this situation, because a duck is easily replaceable for us, however to our local friends and workers the value of a duck is about the same as a week's wage. This gives a little more perspective. Our guards were fully convinced that someone would lose their job because of the missing duck.

Over the next couple of days, each 'worker' approached Tim at individual times to offer their understanding of what had happened, or more cleverly, who was responsible and how they were innocent of wrongdoing. One said, "You know, so and so had family visit him last week. It wouldn't surprise me if he took the duck to feed them." Another commented, "Have you noticed how healthy so and so is looking. It's like he's had extra food to eat." A tangible 'angst' had come over the compound. The usual light mood and easy banter was gone. There was a spirit of suspicion festering. The evidence was strongly pointing toward one particular casual day-worker, although his track record would 'say' otherwise.

When Clayton came to me early one morning in tears, and said, "I have found the duck", it was his pet, after all, he'd hand raised it having watched it hatch. It would follow him around the yard and come when he called it. The whole saga began to unravel. It seems that just before we'd gone away, the missing duck had snuck into our storage shed to find a place to lay her eggs. We had sadly locked her in, and as a result, she had died. Clayton's discovery swept through the compound, the mystery solved but a mess of accusation left hanging. The 'weeks worth of blame and suspicion' among our crew.

This story, like many other real-life events, serve as perfect platforms to teach and demonstrate practical 'kingdom values', and to highlight just how quickly the evil one can trip us up. God has given us a better plan, one of unity, trust and peace.

Our ministry with the Yawo is still at a frontier stage. We are dealing with first-generation believers whose allegiance to Jesus presents constant behaviour choices in daily life. We praise God for the many believers within the Faith Communities and the way they are 'living out' their new faith. They are demonstrating for the next generation just what a follower of Jesus looks like jumping out against the tide.

Chapter 27

CUTE

Malawi

Baba Dayton came to visit us this morning. He is super cute. He'd be horrified if he ever heard me say it. Jarred commented that it was rather an unusual way to describe a man of such age and position in the community. Well, sorry but the fact still remains, he is cute.

The epitome of respect and protocol, he greeted Tim and I. He'd brought some leaves from his garden to feed our rabbits. Just a friendly gesture and an excuse to come and stay connected.

I love how this is still a 'thing' in our community, the 'unannounced visit'. We learnt on our last home assignment, that this was not an acceptable practice in the Australian community anymore. Apparently, two WhatsApp messages at least and a reply plus follow up is required? Anyway cute Baba Dayton was happy to wait while I raced down the hall to change out of my 'wearing around the house weekend attire' and put on my chitenji (wrap/ sarong).

Baba Dayton, when you greet him, always sits lower than you. If you're standing, he'll bow, if you're sitting, he'll kneel and if you're kneeling he'll hunch down on the ground. So awkwardly traditional, Tim and I struggle to adhere to the protocol and we all end up unnaturally perched.

Baba Dayton in his younger days, was a part of the Youth League, a group of young soldiers who served the President, Kamuzu Banda. They would patrol the streets. If you weren't carrying your ID card, they would beat you. If you were caught stealing, they would beat you, if you were accused of disturbing the peace, they would arrest and yes, beat you. Everyone lived in constant fear. I really struggle to see Baba Dayton beating anyone, but I think there is a side of him that he doesn't show to us.

Once a few years ago, we had this strange wind whip up across the community, it was at a critical time in our ministry. Some say it was a spiritual wind. It had a horrific impact. 300 plus houses lost their roofs including our neighbour's flying over our back fence into our yard. Sheets of iron floated around like feathers in the wind. Tim and I already knew what a cyclone feels like, and it certainly felt like one with the wind howling, the leaves and debris whipping across the landscape. It had been completely calm minutes before. Our kids were playing in the yard with their local mates before I'd bundled them all into our house.

We spent the aftermath, storing people's possessions in our garage, helping them keep it safe until they could make a plan to fix their homes. We were soaking wet, muddy and tired. It was night time by now and I still had lots of kids in our house, I needed to get them home to their own families.

Jarred, Clayton and I hopped into the car and crawled our way through the fallen power lines, broken fences and trees across the road. It was pouring rain and very dark. As I drove we saw lines of people heading to the hospital, some with head injuries, others with broken bones and bloodied clothes. It was hard to know who to help or what to do. We did our best and my car was full of people as we escorted them to safety and help.

When we'd dropped off the last child, I looked up to see Baba Dayton waving me down. He'd said God must have sent me because he was heading to us for help. The roof of his house had fallen on his wife. I'd been sent to save her. We joined the long line of patients at the hospital. Her shoulder was dislocated but she would be alright, I assured him what the doctors had said.

As I drove them home, Jarred and Clayton still in the car, I muscled through the muddied roads and obstacles. Tired and a bit defeated, I couldn't see where I was going and in a matter of seconds the entire car hit a bump and was hoisted up wheels spinning in the air, going nowhere. Somehow I managed to hit a tree stump. It caught behind my front wheel and the mudguard, lifted the car so now we sat balanced like a seesaw.

Baba Dayton stood at my window horrified, believing it was all his fault. I pleaded with him that it wasn't and we prayed for wisdom on what to do. Just as I said Amen, I opened my eyes and he was gone. I hopped back in the car and kept trying to rock it from reverse to forward. With the wheels high in the air, this did nothing but more damage underneath. (Sorry Tim) It's funny how often I'd apologize under my breath to Tim for wrecking the car. I guess I was just keeping myself at the moment. Jarred and Clayton still sitting tight in the back seat.

Out of the cover of darkness, we could see figures emerging, one, then two, then four then 10. Suddenly Baba Dayton's face appeared in my window. He'd gone for help. There were maybe 50 people surrounding our car and it took me a few seconds to realize what they were going to do, they were picking us up. They were picking up the entire car and lifting us off the stump. I couldn't believe it. I've never seen such a thing before. Not pushing, lifting. Perhaps I should have counted all the people surrounding my car in the dark and pouring rain because it might be some kind of record.

Baba Dayton had convinced almost all the men in the village and some women too, to come out into the night and the rain and help. I was teary-eyed from emotion and relief, and too tired to personally thank each one of them. Baba Dayton hopped in the front seat smiling like a Cheshire cat. "Let's go, Mama."

Chapter 28
HOME

Australia

I've never been a homebody, a woman who's home is her pride and joy. Being house proud reminds me of the 1950s when being a homemaker was actually listed as an occupation. Don't get me wrong, I like having a nice house to live in, and so far in our married life, we'd lived in 12 houses over 10 years. I've had lots of nice houses and perhaps that's what allows me to hold the houses I've lived in loosely. It's just another building to make a nest in until the next one comes along. Home is where the heart is, and as long as I was with my family I was going to be alright. This is not a reflection on those who dream up their perfect home and spend the rest of their lives making it beautiful. We'd built our business working for these people and I'm glad they exist!

Saying this, when we'd sold up in Cairns and moved to Brisbane, the mission house was only available for 6 months and then we needed to find a place of our own. At the time prices in Brisbane were much higher than prices in Cairns and the fancy home we'd sold in Cairns gave us just enough to buy an ordinary equivalent in Brisbane. We'd searched the internet to find something workable only to have it sold before we could even see it. Our timeline was getting tighter and our search kept leading us to dead ends.

If you've ever been house hunting before, you'll know that it can easily turn quite addictive. Any spare minute becomes an opportunity to look one more time, perhaps you'll stumble across a treasure as you drive home from the shopping centre? Perhaps when you're heading out to work you might discover a hidden suburb sporting the perfect jewel? Would you believe this actually happened for us? One day completely lost in the most beautiful maze of houses we struck gold. The worst house on the best street!

Having just come on the market, we knew in a matter of hours it would be snaffled up in a heartbeat. It had been happening to us all year, we needed to move fast. Tim, who was at college by this time knocked off early and met the real estate agent, offering everything we had. Way under the asking price, it was a long shot at best that it would ever be considered. By that evening the agent had called to say our offer had been rejected. Before hanging up the phone I felt a stirring in my heart and for some reason blurted out that we were heading overseas to Africa and didn't have any more money.

The guy was rather stunned, and instead of hanging up on me, actually, asked if we were people of faith? Weird? Yes, we were! He was silent for a while then asked if we'd mind waiting by the phone for a minute as he wanted to call the owners and get back to us. Can you imagine how much we prayed in those few seconds! Please God, please! True to his word the phone rang and the agent sounded rather excited, his tone completely different from the serious 'Lord Business' a minute ago.

He and the owners went to the same church. They had hesitated about whether selling this house was the right thing to do. They'd met together the night before to pray for a sign that God would guide them in this. Should they jump into this or not? My blurting was their clear answer. We had been sent by God, we were the sign! Tim and I couldn't believe it and neither could they. Our offer was tens of thousands short of their asking price, but they didn't seem to mind. It was all God's money.

By the end of the month, we were ready to move in. It didn't take long because we didn't own much, we'd begged and borrowed mattresses so at least we weren't on the floor, bought a second-hand fridge and then began the scavenger hunt of garage sales to kit out the rest of the house.

Within a week of living there, we received a phone call from Tim's older brother Chris. He and his wife Bron and their daughters Sarah 6 months and Esther 2, had been caught in a tight spot and wondered if our new house could hold two families for 6 months or so. What could we say? Of course, it could. So they moved in downstairs and we lived upstairs. Good thing they are simply awesome people and were just as keen as us to make this work. Did you know God has a funny sense of humour? Of course, you do. The lessons we learned whilst living on top of each other in this house in Brisbane made living in a compound with teammates in Malawi, a piece of cake!

Chapter 29

THE CREST OF THE WAVE

Australia

We left Chris and Bron to hold the fort while we prepared to visit different churches around Queensland, tell our story, ask for support and sponsorship. We hadn't been looking forward to this and with Clayton still suffering we were even more nervous. I'd gotten to the point in my faith however where the impossible seemed within reach. The very house I was living in reminded me that God could, in fact, do anything so it might be worth my while to put in my requests, to just pour out my heart.

'God if you could make all this travelling easier on us, that would be great?' I know God could do anything but would he? Another random phone call proved that he would.

There is an incredible family on the Sunshine Coast, whose daughter's family were our friends in Cairns. They'd been doing some thinking on our behalf and come up with the most wonderful of ideas. Would a caravan help? We could travel all over the place whilst sleeping in the same bed every night. Our constant travel would feel like one long family holiday.

"Meet me down at Jayco Caravans on Saturday." We picked out a brand new 21 foot Jayco Expander with its own toilet and shower. It was like a dream. Our dear friends paid for it, registered it and told us when we were finished and on our way to Malawi, to just drop it back to their place!

The 'Tim and Mel Roadshow' Queensland Tour had begun! 18 months, hundreds of meetings and speaking engagements, 40 plus churches from Cooktown to the Gold Coast over 4000kms. Embracing the mood of our tour, we printed some 'Team Malawi' groupie T-shirts. Building a team of people who would hold the ropes for us, people who would journey with us for the next decade at least. They promised to stand in the gap when we couldn't stand any longer.

God is wonderful and so are his people. I even heard a story of two complete strangers meeting on a beach somewhere in Queensland both on holidays, both wearing a Team Malawi T-shirt. They'd spotted each other and struck up a conversation about how they knew the Downes family. They were on the same team but didn't know each other. God couldn't have been more encouraging if he tried. We were riding on the crest of the wave!

Chapter 30

FAVOUR

Malawi will not let my computer tell me there is no 'u' in favour. There is and it helps me do a little play on words. With God's favour 'you' have to be part of the plan. We have been teaching the beatitudes in the village kids group over the last month or two. God talks a lot about favour or blessings. Most of us don't like to hear it, as suffering, hunger and sadness are not high on our prayer lists.

We are seeing God's favour at the moment in strange little ways and we don't really know why. Has someone been praying for us specifically? Did we do something to please God more than usual?

We are humbled and amazed by this. (And you would be too if you had been to our local markets)

Our water pump had bad oil so it blew a piston. A part you can only get in South Africa. Well, Tim found it in the market the same day!

Our boat has a hole in it and Tim needed to patch it up. He found fibreglass resin at the markets. Unheard of!

Clayton had grown out of his warm jacket and we went to the market to buy a new second hand one (hopefully) I walked in and found one just waiting for us.

It had turned cold and our guesthouse had no blankets. I went in search of and, once again at the markets found what we could afford in perfect condition just sitting there.

We had rats in our roof and garage and despite lots of effort, we could not get rid of them with traps. Well for some strange reason, one lone kitten emerged from under one of the buildings in our compound. (Clayton had been praying for a cat.) Rat problem solved.

A friend of ours was sitting by the road, with a 50kg bag of maize. He'd travelled to town from the village and arrived on the outskirts. He hoped to beg a ride home with his heavy load so he prayed. Tim happened to be driving by with an empty vehicle. Favour won on both sides as they travelled the rest of the journey together.

We had to go to Mozambique for a team meeting. Visas cost nearly $80 USD each. At the border, the guy gave us a 24-hour free pass and told us to save our money. Favour with government officials, now that's just God showing off!

There are other stories that I could add to this, but this list is enough to demonstrate what God does in our lives every day. Proverbs 15:15 says, *"But when you choose to be cheerful, every day will bring you more and more joy and fullness."* Noticing the good always outweighs the bad. We are ever so grateful for all God has given us. It is inspiring to look around and notice what God is doing. He is always doing something.

Chapter 31

JARRED's 10th BIRTHDAY

Malawi

've just walked in the door and showered after a few days away. So nice to be clean! Our week started out of necessity, some time away for regrouping. I think we had been the frog slowly beginning to boil in the pot.

Pride can be a good virtue but it can also be a huge enemy to us. Admitting we need a break is not always how we roll. Our teammates decided that we looked pretty tired which meant that we probably felt twice as bad so we should take some time to go away, to rest and pray.

That we did. Four days away at a simple village house right next to the magnificent Lake Malawi. I sat in a hammock and read whilst the boys played in the lake. Tim tinkered with fixing the water pump and built a fence, (he never sits still anyway) but without the hollering of someone at the door wanting him for a meeting. We were still surrounded by people in the village but they weren't asking anything of us.

I was reading Francine River's "Sons of Encouragement", Aaron's life with Moses and the Israelites leaving Egypt and heading into the Promised Land. The parallels were incredible. Tim's constant meetings with our Yawo friends looked exactly like those between Aaron and Moses and the Israelites. It involved solving disputes and providing for the constant needs around us, praying for discernment as our wisdom and cultural understanding so often fail us.

Nice to know we weren't the first to struggle with such things!

During our time away it was Jarred's birthday. The big 10. Well worth celebrating. So we asked him what he would like to do. Although this sounds like a very open-ended question to give to a nearly 10-year-old boy. Jarred knew that there really aren't that many options here. We could call the few other ex-pat kids from around the region and have a party? Jarred carefully considered the options but returned to us with a suggestion of his own. Mum, Dad I want to take my local friends to the lake for a sleepover.

Since coming here Jarred and Clayton have made friends with our workers' kids, the neighbourhood kids and other randoms who have come by over the years. There is a daily group in our yard wanting to play with the boys. These kids have become part of our lives and it is they who Jarred feels most familiar with.

"I want to take my friends to the lake house and stay there for two whole nights. Could we make sure they eat really well? We could eat meat and rice, buy mandasi (a local doughnut) and maybe even get everyone a Fanta!" So it was decided. Our boy wanted to celebrate with his local friends, so that is what we would do.

We quietly asked 10 of his closest mates to be ready on Friday so we could come back from the lake and pick them up. I went to visit their parents to make the arrangements. It really was quite funny. I could have just taken these children without asking anyone knowing full well that word would have gotten around. But my conscience wouldn't sit well with that. So a personal visit to each child's home was my attempt to show respect and assure the parents that I would care for their child.

I know you are reading this thinking that I am quite sensible in my actions, and for this reassurance I thank you. In my own culture, I am quite rational. Here, however, people humour me and my protocol. Most times I am considered to be either ridiculous, paranoid or ignorant and sometimes all of the above at once!

With the arrangements made, we arrived Friday morning, ready to pick up more supplies, my local friend Del (who is my Malawian Catering Queen) and the 10 children we had organized.

Sounds simple right? Makes logical sense and should work to plan, right? We were so, so wrong!

Our quiet word wasn't kept all that quiet. We had every kid from almost everywhere all waiting in our compound. Jarred came into our house horrified, "Mum there are hundreds of kids out there and lots that I've never even seen before!"

O.K. there weren't hundreds of kids, a slight exaggeration, but there were lots of kids we hadn't seen before and most of them we definitely hadn't invited.

So here arises our first cultural issue. Obviously, word had gotten around of Jarred's lake party. The wisdom of the Yawo was to send in the kids to appeal to our generosity and soft-heartedness. Things had been organized so that we were made to feel bad if we said no. Crying children and upset parents expected that us rich whites should cave to the pressure. Jarred's birthday party had become a political and cultural standoff.

10-year-old boys generally don't have to deal with such pressure. Jarred was overwhelmed with all the kids surrounding him begging for his attention and wanting his 'friendship'.

Not wanting to upset anyone, he retreated into the house bursting into tears. "I don't know what to do?"

We gathered for a family meeting. Tim asked Jarred to write down the names of his 10 friends. The plan was only those would come the rest would be sent home, in tears if necessary. We walked back out to load things into the car and for the first time, I recognized what was going on. Oh no! Cultural issue number two. The local ladies I have been working hard to make connections with and minister to had sent their kids along.

We gathered again, this time for a 'parents only' meeting. Tim and I discussed the repercussions of rejecting these kids and how that would that affect our ministry. We gave our opinion to Jarred who agreed that now the birthday list should have more names on it.

Out we went again, but with the plan not to enter into negotiations. The Yawo love negotiations and can cleverly manipulate any situation. We held out for as long as possible. By this time, some of the extras had got the hint that they weren't overly welcome. So our numbers had dropped a bit.

Tim began to load certain children into the car. We did a headcount; our ten kids had become 20. The Troupe Carrier was overflowing, yet there were still kids trying to get in. I shut the door only to have other children run after us crying out. It was a horrible situation to be in.

Cultural issue number three- compassion versus common sense. We were maxed out at 20 kids, so enough was enough. Off we went.

There is a big difference between entertaining 10 kids all Jarred's age to organizing 20 kids ranging from 2 years to 17. Fortunately for us, Tim and I had had many years under our belts of running kids camps, so Jarred's birthday party evolved into a Malawian children's camp.

We split the kids into groups, began playing my adapted Aussie games into their Yawo equivalent. Tug of war went well, races always a winner, three-legged races worked but ended in injury. Teamwork activities, a scavenger hunt and lots of swimming seemed to tide us over. Tim introduced a bar of soap, to spice things up. Swimming became bathing. (Such a good idea, as I am sure these kids had been wearing the same clothes all week in the 40-degree heat!)

The next morning we had all risen, eaten breakfast and played our first few games by 6.30am. It was a long day. Fortunately, Mama Del my dear friend and catering queen converted the 5 loaves and 2 fish into enough food for us all, plus the day guard, the night guard, the caretaker and his son.

The lollies we'd bought became points for each game. The kids were surprisingly well behaved and all looked after each other. It was nothing to see a 17-year-old boy walking around with a 2-year-old child on his back. I guess living in community is extremely normal in village life. My confidence in the sit-

JARRED'S 10TH BIRTHDAY

uation settled. Until the evening when we realized we only had 6 beds between 20 kids, Jarred and Clayton among them.

Again only in Malawi, would this not present itself a problem. Most kids come from mud huts and sleep only on a mat anyway. Sharing a mattress was not a problem. Somewhere in all the bodies was Jarred, arms and legs entangled, all boys snoring away. Clayton, however, decided that Mum and Dad's bed looked like a better option. You can't blame him really.

It took a good lot of courage for Jarred to embrace this weekend. Despite the tears and overwhelming influx, he pulled himself together, shared everything he had, (and then some) and made sure his friends had a good time. His 10th birthday party was one we remember. Watching our boy show such good character was definitely a proud parent moment. I pray he won't need too much counselling later on in life.

A few days later back at home after the party, Jarred joined in our family devotion. His memory verse: Philippians 4:4 Rejoice in the Lord always, and I say it again rejoice.

He gave me a paper bag with " Blessing Bag" written on the side, it was full of small pieces of paper each one holding a blessing.

1. Life
2. Cool bikes
3. A very, very, very, very cool brother
4. A way to heaven through Jesus
5. Good holidays
6. The Bible
7. A car
8. A cool birthday
9. Lots of toys
10. A pet rabbit
11. Nice home
12. A television.
13. An iPad given to us from a church in Australia.
14. Good health
15. Friends in Africa.

After reading these, I welled up. The best birthday present is the ability to be thankful for what we already have. Here was Jarred counting his blessings the same afternoon his party finished. He had received no presents from his friends. He spent most of his time trying to create unity between the kids and maintain enthusiasm for the games we played even if most didn't know what was going on. He shared all his possessions, including his food (beans, rice and beef), clothes, bed, sheets and pillow. His birthday cake was gone in a frenzy, seconds after the lame attempt of singing 'Happy Birthday'. (Very difficult to sing if no one knows the words or the tune.) He wasn't made to feel special at all. In fact, he felt the impact of being clearly the odd one out.

The cultural issues he faced that weekend are debated in lecture halls, universities and colleges without an answer. Yet Jarred at 10 has learnt to roll with it. We frequently face cultural controversy. Tim and I constantly wrestled with life issues that are contrary to our own worldview. We were the odd ones out and worked hard at bridging the wide gap. Watching our kids wrestle with the same issues was tough, yet it seemed that it was all a matter of perspective.

I asked if I could borrow Jarred's Blessing Bag sometime. With a quick nod of his head and a smile, he said, "Sure Mum, anytime." Then rolled over in bed, another day done.

May God grant me the serenity to accept the things I cannot change, the courage to change the things I can and the wisdom to know the difference.

Happy Birthday Jarred we are so proud of you!

Chapter 32

BLIND BLESSINGS

Malawi had a very sore eye. It was simply some dust blowing into my eye, which turned nasty. It became so painful that I couldn't sleep. Every movement caused irritation that let me think of nothing else.

In the middle of the night in lots of pain and frustration, I woke Tim to pray for me. When morning came, we went to the local hospital to see if there was anyone there who could help.

After some searching, we found that the Eye Specialist from Blantyre (nearest big city) was visiting. Tim was able to speak to him and arranged a consultation.

I was half-blind with only one eye working at this stage. Not being able to see properly was to be my saving grace. There were people everywhere, queuing out into the car park. The hospital Outpatients was always like this. People came from everywhere before sunrise in the hope to see a doctor. Many sleep in the hospital grounds and cook on an open fire. Those who were admitted must come with a guardian. Someone who will feed, wash and care for them the entire time they were in hospital. There were no facilities for these guardians who generally sleep on the floor of the hospital or outside on the ground where it is cooler. Many struggle to find the funds to buy food and cook it. Firewood, maize flour and some kind of relish like Chinese cabbage or beans must be purchased. Most folk living in villages would grow this in their gardens to feed their families, but living in town forces them to find money they don't have.

We opened the door to an ordinary crowded room with people standing shoulder to shoulder waiting to see the specialist who was huddled in a corner. Nothing was private in this hospital. It was expected that those who waited should turn a blind eye rather than those vulnerable hiding themselves. This concept was crucial to how people live in close proximity yet maintain privacy. There often is no private place to retreat to, so there's a common understanding that you just don't look. If you did happen to see something by mistake, then you pretended that you didn't so you wouldn't humiliate the vulnerable person. Bathing areas by the lake, sleeping arrangements in the villages and hospitals all operate with this understanding. Privacy is given not taken.

As the door opened in this waiting room it bumped into a person standing directly behind. We shuffled in through the gap. It was darker than the hallway, and smelt like a room full of very hot people who had been waiting there for a long time!

Being blind in one eye helped me stay respectful, I was watching Tim's feet and keeping my head down, a cloth held over my sore eye trying to protect it. Tim turned to direct me into the room in a culturally appropriate manner. As he did so he whispered in my ear, "Whatever you do, don't look."

"Don't look where?" was my first thought. I couldn't really see anything but people, but now that he'd told me not to look, I really wanted to. Keeping my head down, I knew that I shouldn't ask Tim any more questions with so many people around. It would appear rude. The minutes went by and my good eye adjusted to the dim light. I could hear the doctor speaking in the corner to a patient. Eventually, a few people left and the room rearranged itself for the next patient to come forward. A space had opened up and there, only a metre away from me, behind the door I saw what Tim was talking about.

The person we bumped into was actually a surgeon operating on someone's eye in the same room as us and all the other people! The patient was under general anesthetic with white sheets over them, except the part where the eye operation was happening! We could see everything, actually, the entire room could see everything. It felt like I was conducting the operation myself, or at least assisting. My stomach turned, I've never been good with such things. So I shut both eyes and prayed until it was my turn to see the doctor.

Chapter 33

WELCOME

Malawi

We have a lot of visitors for a lot of different reasons. People visiting from Australia coming to see the work, those travelling through needing a bed for the night, others living in country but needing some encouragement and socialization. Not many weeks go by without someone staying. Our compound has been known for years as Grand Central Station, always alive with people coming and going. If not expatriates, our local friends come daily for a chat or to sort an issue, for prayer or to just hang out. Like an oasis, it acts as a source of security for many, a place where they can safely come and find love, belonging, acceptance and authentic relationships.

We have worked hard over the years to create this dynamic. There is a very different vibe inside the walls to the rest of the community and we work hard to keep it that way. Kingdom values rule, from the kids bouncing in, to the old night guards, we all need each other. Issues are not swept under the carpet, we don't gossip, we try not to judge or put others down nor do we take advantage of someone less fortunate than ourselves. Clear healthy boundaries help us all live in peace and it is attractive. Many come to experience the peace that is found here.

One of my favourite parts of life is being able to watch someone take a leap of faith. When I get to stand next to them and encourage them to jump. For many of our short-term volunteers, simply landing at the airport is a stretch way beyond their comfort zone, let alone living here with us. We often say coming to Africa is just one big self-help program. If we are lucky we might contribute in some way to a lasting change in the community, but mostly we are the ones doing the learning. The jumping. Hosting so many visitors, we've been the launch pad for many willing to put themselves out there, ask God the big questions and find direction. It is a delight to witness God giving strength and courage to those willing to ask.

Duné had volunteered her Gap Year to serve with us. She had come on an adventure, bravely jumping out of her comfort zone for six months. As we picked her up from the airport in the city, we had to apologize. The following few hours were to be taken up running errands, finding plumbing parts and pipe pieces. She did well, jetlagged, yet going with the flow!

The next morning Duné and I spent some time discussing the spiritual implications of her coming, and the pattern of 'testing' that generally happened to all those who visited. As a rule, something would go wrong, something would happen out of the ordinary that would challenge her and test her resolve. We prayed over her, prayed diligence and reliance on God, and we asked God for his guidance when the time of testing came. She needed to be aware that this was a normal part of the journey. It helped us all to prepare our hearts and minds. God was always in control even if we weren't. Trusting in his purpose was a comfort.

We began the journey home but had to be sidetracked with yet another hour or two of errands, sorting out issues at the Road Traffic Department. Instead of all of us waiting in queues for hours, I sent Jarred and Clayton off with Duné to a nearby creek, a nicer way to spend the time.

Sometimes I don't like it when I am right and this is one of those moments. Duné's test came only hours after our discussion. I saw her limping back having been gone for 10 minutes or so. Duné was a mess, emotional, shaken and upset. I gave Jarred and Clayton a questioning look to which they just shrugged their shoulders. They didn't know what she was so upset about. I left my place in the queue and took her to a shaded tree. Comforting her I sat quietly until she was able to tell me the story.

She had been full of wonder and excitement at this new adventure, she wasn't looking where she was walking and had simply tripped over a rock. A small graze on her knee wasn't the source of her grief. In her shaking hand, she revealed the issue. Her iPhone completely smashed. Poor thing, what a way to begin her time here! An 18-year-old Australian millennial without a phone in the middle of Africa. What could be worse! Bless her heart, she was trying to be strong, she was trying to remember what we had talked about that morning but I could see that this was a low blow. We prayed together and took some deep breaths. There was no quick solution to this problem that I could see. God, however, was not slow to answer.

Minutes after her fall, Duné's mother happened to call my phone from Western Australia. She had called Head Office, who had called Tim, who had given my number, which she then rang. God's timing was perfect and Mum was able to love her over the phone. Thank you, Lord! It was simply wonderful to watch Duné over the next six months. She came to Malawi a young girl but after listening to God and learning from all that he had for her, she left a confident woman ready to jump again.

Chapter 34

INITIATION CELEBRATIONS

Malawi

It was Initiation time again. My friend with twin girls invited me to the celebration of their 'coming out'. There were celebrations all over; we went to sleep most nights to the sound of drums beating over the fence on the airstrip. It was a special time, and of course, I went on this occasion to bless and encourage these girls whom I had known all their life.

As part of the process the children who had been in a hut for the last month, learning about growing up and how to be an adult, were ceremonially washed and specially dressed. Both the boy's and girl's groups join for the 'coming out' celebration. It was a very significant time in a Yawo person's life. You are not truly Yawo if you haven't been through initiation. Boys were circumcised and so were the girls in the past. Thank goodness for the girls it's now outlawed but the boys still undergo a crude interaction with a razor blade and some methylated spirit. It's a heavy spiritual time that lasts for a month or so. Those in charge practice traditional African medicine with chants and rituals to protect the children from evil spirits. It is a liminal time of transition, a time of confusion and often fear for the children as well as a time of learning combined with celebration.

I arrived with Duné who was still with us at this point and waited with the others who gathered. We ate Ugali (maize porridge) together, then were ushered to another house to eat yet again. We were being honoured. I was asked if we would mind using our car to pick up the children who were quite a distance away at their special hut. Of course, I didn't mind and had actually brought the Troupe Carrier just for this purpose. We drove about 10km to the children, a dozen or so of them, and then another dozen or so more adults and helpers piled into the car. With doors open and people hanging out of every window, we were met by a crowded procession dancing to the drums. They surrounded the car and paraded with us like a street festival to the ceremonial site.

Four hours later, we snuck out of the frenzy, dust in our teeth, sweat sticking our shirts to our back, ears ringing from the singing and dancing. It is not for the faint-hearted. We left them to dance into the night. Our hearts were heavy. These days the ceremony is changing. The dancing looks more like a Beyoncé film clip with alcohol often in the mix than the traditional Yawo celebration. The western influence was obvious; teenagers were keen to move away from the traditions of their ancestors.

New believers wrestle with this as it has both positive and negative consequences. They needed to stay involved. We need to encourage believers to find a new narrative that honours tradition and God at the same time. We need to hold their hand as they challeng the status quo and jump to defend the next generation.

Chapter 35

~~~

ELEPHANTS

Malawi

It's not very often we act the tourist. Not many of us bother with the local sights and sounds of the place we call home. Mostly we escort our visitors when they come, but we rarely find the time to enjoy all Malawi has to offer. A stunning country mostly taken up by a freshwater lake, it boasts beautiful undulating mountains, tea estates from the colonial days, untouched villages and rich culture.

During the wet season, the entire scene transforms from a hot dusty wasteland to a lush green bursting with life. It is a land of contrasts, a raw beauty that allures the visitor into a sense of wonder. Despite unseen dangers, most holidaymakers spend their time here in luxury. There are enough lodges and tourist locations to make a seriously good impression. I remember one tourist asking me if I could take her to see the poor people living in poverty, another wanted me to show him people suffering from malaria. The distance between the tourists and real Malawian life makes it hard not to be frustrated at such requests.

Nearby to us, is Liwonde National Park. It is teeming with wildlife and boasts the Big Five. According to Wikipedia, in Africa, the Big Five game animals are the lion, leopard, rhinoceros, elephant, and Cape buffalo. The term was coined by big-game hunters, and refers to the five most difficult animals in Africa to hunt on foot, but is now also widely used by safari tour operators as a 'must-see' when visiting.

We had the opportunity of a lifetime. We had been invited to help capture five hundred elephants that needed to be relocated from this National Park to another National Park up north. We had made friends with the game ranger, Lawrance and his family, who let us know about this incredible project. We transformed from cross-cultural workers into adventurers on safari.

There we were right in the middle of it all. Helicopters were flying overhead, shooting tranquillizer darts, the vet and game rangers tending to the elephants and loading them onto trucks. Jarred and Clayton were given two tranquillized elephants each to monitor. They had to put sticks in their trunks to keep their airways open and listen to their breathing by resting their ears on the chests of the sleeping giants.

Tim was a runner, pushing over the darted elephants so they would land on their side and not suffocate. He'd ignorantly worn a red t-shirt instead of khaki. A big mistake when dealing with live game, he would not blend into the surrounding environment. He became known as 'Big Red' as the project coordinator hollered orders. We painted numbers on the elephants to determine which one was which. A crane hoisted them onto the waiting trucks and into the holding containers. It was fascinating and incredibly exciting. We were lost in a completely different world. It reminded me of Jurassic Park. We had to pinch ourselves to be sure what was happening around us was real. This kind of jumping was fantastic, such adventure, such fun!

The project went on for several months and was promoted worldwide, you can Google it if you like. It is quite famous, but you won't find us anywhere in the photos. You will, however, find Prince Harry. He arrived the week after us. Poor guy, imagine having to fill our shoes!

Chapter 36

BUZZ

Australia and Malawi

It had been three years of preparation, travel, meetings and closure that saw us standing with our suitcases in the airport. Our family was swarming around us in a buzz of sadness and excitement. This was it. This was what we'd been working towards. We were actually doing it. We were as ready as we were ever going to be. Malawi here we come! Jarred just now five years old and Clayton nearly three holding onto his precious Dolly, waved goodbye one more time to their doting grandparents. This was the turn of a page and the beginning of a new chapter in our lives. Things were never going to be the same again. We were leaving all we had ever known heading out on this great adventure.

Clayton, however, was still a sick little boy. We'd spent a lot of time at the hospital in the emergency room with his newly developed asthma. He lived now with chest infections that just wouldn't budge. He couldn't get an all-clear for his medical. Our doctor claimed after three courses of antibiotics that Clayton was as good as he was going to get. We'd been told dozens of times by well-meaning individuals that we were being irresponsible taking our children into deepest darkest Africa. It hurt to be judged. It was hard to stand tall when I knew the truth to what they were saying. We were taking a huge risk, a leap of faith. We were jumping. I agree that it wasn't really a logical idea, but God had asked us to obey so our life was in his hands.

We touched down at the Malawi International Airport which was more like a big shed. Our new team leader met us. He took us to a guesthouse to sleep off our jetlag before we headed that very next morning the Department of Transport or Road Traffic as it's known here. We queued with a swarm of hundreds of other people, huddling in the sun for three days to get our Malawian driving licenses. It was a rude introduction. Patience was a lesson to be learnt over and over again. Lucky us!

Three hours drive brought us to our new home. It was in a compound surrounded by high brick walls, night guards, barred windows and locked doors. Malawians were buzzing everywhere they greeted us and unloaded our boxes. I'd never had so much help in my life. I wasn't allowed to carry anything. The house had been set up beautifully with a welcome sign and a meal waited for us. It was a strange mix of comfort and contrast.

The Gastroenterologist had explained that if Clayton was going to grow out of his allergies, it would most likely be between the ages of three and five years. We'd been in Malawi a month when the inevitable happened. We had learned to make rice milk from scratch, we'd been preparing for an allergic flare-up knowing that we wouldn't have the range of food available to us. We'd been proactive. We'd been careful. But Jarred left his cup of full cream dairy milk on the table and before we could stop him, Clayton had reached for it and downed the lot. Tim and I panicked waiting for his lips to swell, his pain to begin, his skin to turn red. We froze, we watched and waited. We'd kept Clayton away from dairy for the last 18 months. How could we have been so careless? We were in the middle of Africa, what were we going to do?

Clayton with his chubby cheeks and huge almond eyes sat and just looked back at us puzzled. His lips didn't swell, his skin didn't turn red and his pain didn't come. It never came. From that day on Clayton could drink milk, eat wheat bread and pretty much scoff anything he wanted. His eczema disappeared, his digestion was pain-free. He was a completely different child.

Chapter 37

TESTING

Malawi

I mentioned earlier that jumping can make you feel very vulnerable. It's a time of testing and waiting on God to catch you. Most of the time we live without knowing the backstory, without knowing what had happened before we landed. Jumping means leaving one place and entering another. For us arriving in Malawi was nothing like we'd thought it would be.

Between our new team members, there had been tension, there had been conflict and there wasn't a lot of love being shared. Tim and I joked that you could cut the air with a knife during our team gatherings. There were so many elephants in the room we could hardly move. We hadn't been told the whole story and now that we had arrived in Malawi, people were being careful to hide the truth from us. No one wanted their dirty laundry displayed, and who can blame them. They were all good people doing the best they could in very difficult circumstances.

We ignorantly asked questions. We made offensive efforts of reconciliation and we lived most of the time with one big foot in our mouth. Ignorance was not bliss and our being in Malawi was not met with a lot of enthusiasm, by the rest of the struggling team.

Conflict is not unusual in teams, especially ones that have lived through hardship and tragedy. Team conflict is the second reason as to why most cross-cultural workers leave the field. (Children's education is the first.) In cross-cultural work stress is off the charts, tension, feelings of being overwhelmed and outnumbered are all contributors to why there is conflict. Burnout, compassion fatigue and depression with psychosomatic illnesses were all commonplace in our industry. We'd arrived into a team barely held by a few strands of unity. We'd later found out that Tim and I were hoped to be the glue to hold everyone together. It would have been nice to know this before we packed up our lives and moved here.

One family was concluding their time of service. They were very friendly to us as newcomers and spent a lot of time grooming us to align with their strategies. When Tim was on an orientation village trip with them, he felt a coolness enter the conversation. Tim was asking too many questions and his enquiry was not welcomed. We were to find out that bullying and abuse was a method of persuasion often used by those under stress. This was one occasion where a volcano of abuse erupted. Being called all sorts of names and ending with the direction for us to go back to Australia. It was hard to hear that we were not wanted.

Tim was stunned but not rattled. Who'd have thought that 10 years on a building site dealing with sub-contractors was fantastic preparation for working on a dysfunctional team? We decided that this unnecessary behaviour was not going to unnerve us or our calling. Tim was able to calm them down and explain that we needed some space and that perhaps they should focus more on the task at hand and caring for their own family. Their response was full of tears and regret. They were seriously suffering from lack of stability.

We were taken aback. Was this what was going to happen to us? Were we going to be rattled and become so unstable? Grieved and disappointed we spent the remaining weeks defending ourselves and trying to remain positive about what God was going to do. We watched as each team member struggled with their own demons. We prayed for healing. We cried out to God for protection. Was this our future too?

I can liken what we felt to the story written in the bible about Daniel. He described a Prince of Persia that rested over the region. This Prince exerted spiritual oppression. It rested heavily on our shoulders and we watched it torment others. This spiritual force had a right to be here, and we were not welcomed. More than ever before we were outnumbered, we'd brought a knife to a gunfight. We were not ready for the spiritual battle we'd been placed in.

Our honeymoon phase of living in utopia was very short-lived. We were going to have to be tough. We were going to have to be savvy and we were going to have to grow a very thick skin in this new world and put on our spiritual armour so that we landed on solid ground. We had to believe with all our hearts that God would fight for us and claiming his promise was our sword and shield.

Chapter 38

THE PRODIGAL SON

Malawi

Often we translate meanings from bible stories through our own cultural filters. The Prodigal Son is a story we all knew well. Tim and I discussed the story together before I went to Ladies Group to teach it. The main points we thought were obvious, rebellion, Sonship (the son didn't ever stop being a son), and repentance.

As we went through the story, the ladies were very vocal about their meaning behind the story. "It is a story about parenting. The father accepted the son back without rebuke and didn't beat him. We should also accept our children back after they have rebelled against us and not beat them. That's why if you beat them you can be taken to the police.

The pigs are not real pigs (because who in their right mind would ever keep pigs?) They represent evil spirits like anger, hate, hunger and fear. All are tormenting the son and haunting him in his dreams. He has no peace. The last part is about jealously. The big brother was jealous and most likely put a curse on the younger brother.

The ladies said that we all get jealous so easily and are tempted to use manipulation on others, but in the end, it ruins us. If the story continued the big brother would be the one back with the pigs because of the jealously in his heart. Using evil to fight evil is what we've always done. But God is telling us here to let him take control. We need to trust him to fight for us.

So yet again it turns out I was the learner in this situation, I knew very little of the spirit world and didn't have much to say at all. My passion for finding out about spirituality in the bible was ignited. I had so much to learn.

Chapter 39

CRY

Malawi

I just wanted to sit and cry. Sometimes we think we can mask the truth with excuses. Excuses that we make up for other people explaining their actions so that it doesn't hurt us so much. Well, this day the truth just came smashing through. Our guard had just walked in to tell me something. He was angry, not angry with me however angry with his wife, my good friend and angry with the other ladies I knew.

The ladies group had been going forever but lately, the group had been rather sparse. Only a few ladies came each week. Enough to keep us going but certainly not any representation of those who have attended over the years.

Our guard stood before me furious at these women. "Mama, you are always loving these ladies, helping them when they need it, encouraging them, looking after their kids, you are so consistent and reliable. Yet they treat you terribly."

He unpacked how he'd watched me each week. I had visited the sick, I had prayed with those who were sad, I gave to the needy, I was the first one the ladies came to when there were problems. "Yet when things were good, where were they?" he said. They weren't coming to pray because they weren't suffering. They don't need you so they don't come.

Suddenly my heart weighed a ton. I kind of knew this was happening but didn't want to admit it. The truth was staring me in the face. Compared to the other things in their lives, I was not so interesting. God's word wasn't as exciting to them as it first was. Distractions, busyness, priorities were all to blame for the lack of commitment. When things were good, you didn't need God, or Mama Mel so it seemed.

"Mama you are loving them but they aren't loving you. They do love you but they aren't showing it as they should be." How beautiful that he wanted to share this with me. His honesty was filling the gap in my heart that had just opened up a little wider.

So there you go. I was the nerdy kid at school with no friends apparently. I was the one who was trying to fit in, trying to show love and cross the massive barriers of culture and language. Despite all our history, the stories of the amazing things God had done, the miracles we'd seen together, the breakthroughs, the answered prayers were forgotten so quickly. Well, perhaps not forgotten, but certainly overlooked.

As I sat down I just had to vent. I had to feel sorry for myself just for a minute. Then, I had to do the same old steps I'd done a thousand times and would have to do a thousand times again. I forgave them and I repented. I forgave these friends of mine because they didn't know what they were doing. They were not malicious and mean. They weren't spiteful or nasty. They were just ordinary people. Ordinary people just like me, which is why I had to repent because I was no different. I'm selfish, I'm greedy, I'm self-righteous and judgmental. I get distracted and busy and I get my priorities wrong. I could not point the finger. And apparently, as I read my bible, this was not a new story. God sits and waits to get our attention so I needed to repent of that too.

Don't you just love how God uses our hurts to remind us just how hurtful we are to him?

'God help me to remain patient and continue showing love even when it isn't being reciprocated. I'm sorry for the number of times I have done this to you! You who have called me to be obedient and faithful help me to endure and fill me with your love that never runs out!' Amen

Chapter 40

RAMADAN RANDOMS

Malawi

It never ceases to amaze us the weird things that happen here during Ramadan. One year Ramadan had only just begun and already there were some beauties.

Tim had gone to the bank. (That is not the interesting part, but rather the opposite as going to the bank often means long waits and not always positive results!)

Just say he intended to leave to go the bank at 9am (I'm guessing because I actually don't remember the time.) But he was interrupted and so left a few minutes later at 9.15am.

Some would call this just pure luck. Others would take this as a direct answer to those people praying for our safety. Those 15 minutes made a big difference. As Tim pulled up into the bank car park, he was met with a dramatic scene. Blood was splattered everywhere, guts sprawled over the ground and 50 odd people were trapped inside the bank looking desperately through the window. 15 minutes before a rabid dog (a dog with rabies) went mad on the steps of the bank. It was so out of control that the 'local government game warden' (who normally shoots problem hippos and crocodiles) was called to shoot the dog.

The second story happened just today. On the way to the village group, Tim passed through the markets. Normally bustling with people it was like a ghost town. A shoe, bags, parcels, food, mats all left where they stood but not a soul was around. What had happened here? Had the rapture happened without us?

No, a swarm of bees randomly took over the market and scattered the hundreds of people into hiding.

Another day...."Ngwena, Ngwena" people were running, a huge crowd was forming. What is going on? Tim had walked into the crowd asking the question. They didn't have to wait long. There in front of him was a guy with blood pouring down his arm pooling on his lap. He was sitting on a bike ready to be taken to hospital. He made no sound, he was pale and wide-eyed. There were no fingers on the hand he held, just stumps of where they used to be. He set fish traps for a living and this time it cost him his fingers. Crocodiles are common where we live, sometimes we forget that there wasn't the luxury of choice for most people. Working alongside dangers is just part of life.

Also this week, in the flow of conversation, Tim asked an older lady in the village group, "When you were younger, were there lions here?" Sometimes, we don't know what we are asking. She looked at Tim strangely. "Yes Baba, my oldest son was killed by a lion. That's his grave there!"

Then we found Clayton's cat sprawled out on the ground. We rescued it only to watch it die. Who knows from what? That very same evening when we were expecting dinner guests (our Australian guest speakers for the team retreat), Jarred walked into the house leading Clayton who was blind with a face full of dirt and blood. He'd been playing chasey with his local mates and fallen off the fence literally biting the dust. Tim entertained our guests while I cleaned up Clayton assessing the damage. No stitches needed but lots of gravel rash. His eyes were fine. His lips were blowing up like a balloon but no teeth were busted. He spent the next week drinking from a straw.

The following, Clayton was sick with fevers. The doctor explained that Clayton was run down and lacking nutrition from not eating enough. I was horrified! Is this what a terrible mother feels like? He was growing almost an inch a month at the time and wasn't all that hungry with his sore mouth.

Are these events just coincidences? Or are they part of the unseen battle. A battle that rages around us? We don't pray into an empty space, even if it feels like it some days. Our prayers matter. They are heard. They tip the balance and guard our hearts against the hopelessness.

Chapter 41
∞
STRANGE

Malawi

Lots of strange things were normal nowadays. So normal that we don't call such events strange anymore. An event like a rabid dog being shot at the bank was just a good story for the dinner table. But what I'm about to tell you tends to fit into a different category. This type of event is one that everyone knows is happening but no one talks about. They pretend it isn't happening because it's easier to go with the flow. It is easier to let sleeping dogs lie, those who stick their necks out generally get it chopped off. Those who jump by speaking up can get hurt in the process.

Tim and I launched wholeheartedly into language learning. Four hours a day for the first few years and then for the rest of our lives. We discovered that we would never stop learning this language. We were studying for an exam that came every day as long as we lived here. It certainly wasn't a pretty journey. I always felt there was a stronghold in the process. People felt it impossible to learn. Many had tried and failed. Many didn't want us to learn it as it opened too many doors, an Asungu (foreigner) speaking and understanding Ciyawo would give far too much insight into the cultural current driving the ripples most see on the surface.

We could be seen as spies uncovering hidden secrets in these ancient people and complicated community.

The language, Ciyawo had a stigma as a primitive language, the village language. A Bantu language boasting of nine noun classes, intricate tenses and sound changes. We saw it as a comprehensive study of the mind, body and soul. Communication did open a way into a person's motivations. Learning this language was leading a way to connect with its people.

It was early days when visitors from Australia came to tour the projects run by our organization. N.G.O's (Non-Government Organisations) or aid and development organisations and international charities are everywhere in Malawi. They come with an agenda of helping those less fortunate. They come with well-meaning experts, those usually with their academic doctorates or masters in aid and development. They promote sustainable practices for long term solutions of things like food security, reforestation, community development incentives, adult literacy and savings clubs. It is a big business. Statistics say that most of Malawi's national income originates from these programs, outside donors coming to rescue those in need.

Without sounding too cynical, these programs are largely donor-driven, those giving the money decide what should happen with it. They are outside visitors coming into a community and dictating what the biggest needs are and then developing a program to fix those needs. The developing world provides the perfect platform for this massive worldwide industry.

The group from Australia had come to see up close and personal the projects our organization was running in the village. They wanted to see where their money had gone. They wanted to meet those whose lives they had saved. It was a feel-good trip and Tim and I were joining in. We piled into the tour bus and bounced around the villages, using an interpreter supplied by our N.G.O. We were introduced to the village chiefs and those on the coal face. We watched as the chiefs spoke and the interpreter using his most eloquent English unpacked the details of each project. We were shown fish farming, bridge building, kitchen gardens and reforestation. The entire day was smooth, well put together and highly impressive.

In the quietness of the evening, Tim and I wrestled with what we saw. From our little time with our language helpers and our own private village visits, something wasn't adding up. The second day of our tour presented the same slick presentation. This time Tim and I listened harder to what the chief spoke in Ciyawo. We introduced ourselves to the local bystanders and tried to ask some more questions. What we uncovered over the remainder of this tour was a monster, a mighty sleeping giant that was going to destroy us. We kept it to ourselves. If what we suspected was right, we would need hard evidence. We would need proof. We would need to do research and reports over the coming months. We needed surveys and statistics to back up our discoveries.

We dared not speak of this to anyone. We worked hard at reading between the lines. We were piecing together the puzzle. Months went by, we prayed, we asked God for guidance. Should we speak out or should we let sleeping dogs lie? What would be the future for us if this story got out? The restlessness increased as it does when you sit on a secret for a long period of time. The secret was like cancer eating its way into our soul.

We decided to make a plan. We put together a report with testimonies from other local believers and our Australian team members and presented it to our leadership in Australia. We needed to do what was right even if it meant people got hurt in the process. We had to report what we'd found out. Our entire development N.G.O program was a scam.

It may be a surprise to you, but corruption in Africa is not unusual. What was unusual in this situation was that it was happening on our shift, right in front of our nose and we hadn't seen it, our organization hadn't seen it. People were being paid off left right and centre. Smooth operators were lying outright in the reports to the donors. From the Malawian management in the office to the local fieldworkers in the village, everyone was in on it. Everyone was getting a piece of the pie. It was an 'us and them' mentality, we take the donors money and pocket it, whilst telling them what they want to hear, stroking their egos, allowing them to feel the hero.

Our organization had no idea what was really going on. It had been going on for such a long period of time that it was seen to be normal. Tim and my fresh eyes saw a different story and in our idealistic ignorance, thought we would be rewarded for our efforts.

We were definitely not rewarded. Those who had been pocketing the donors' money were angry, very angry. We were receiving regular death threats. They were going to poison our children. They were going to ruin our lives. We had to pay for police protection. Our organization was looking for a way to remove us quietly. We felt vulnerable, unsupported and our lives were in danger. We were sworn to secrecy. We felt alone.

In the middle of this storm, we received a phone call from home. My Dad had been taken to the hospital. He'd been diagnosed with terminal bowel cancer and hadn't been given long to live. It was all too much; the attacks were coming too quickly and for too long. Tim had taken to travelling to the villages with police sporting guns and tear gas for protection. I was broken. I wasn't strong enough to win this fight. I was being hit from every direction and left crawling through no man's land. This battle wasn't against flesh and blood. We knew it with all our hearts. God had asked us to stand up and shine a light. Would I still hold it?

I had every reason in the world for giving up. I was asked to give up, I was threatened if I didn't. But I couldn't, God wouldn't let me. He had asked me to jump, he'd asked me to follow in his footsteps even if it meant my life, the life of my family. Oh how I wrestled with him, how angry I was. How frustrated and twisted I felt that doing the right thing had cost me so dearly.

Then I saw his face. The one on the cross, giving his life for mine. He wasn't asking me to do anything harder than what he'd already done. He hadn't asked me to fix this mess, he asked me to hold on to him. So I held on with every fiber of my being, just like those giants of the faith who had gone before me. If ever I needed you to catch me, God, it was now!

Our situation didn't miraculously go away. It took months before our names were cleared and the organization saw the situation for what it was. The entire

N.G.O was shut down, leadership resigned, the mess was cleaned up, the battle was over but the war raged on. We were left standing, a small group of us, those who had stood their ground. We were wounded and we were tired but we were hopeful.

Chapter 42

NORMAL

Malawi

It's a strange concept that I heard articulated well when we were reading the Bryce Courtney book, The Power of One. It explained how if you do anything long enough it starts to feel normal and perfectly natural, even the weirdest and the most dramatic of events.

When we first arrived, I was completely spun out. Everything looked like it came straight out of a World Vision advertisement, village huts, markets, roads full of people. Women carrying parcels on their heads, children dressed in rags playing in the dirt. It was hard to see past the stigma that was attached to these images. Not only was I seeing this in real life, but it was now my job to live amongst these people, not just send money to some faraway place. My adrenaline peaked with an emergency call. A friend was dying. Can we go and take them to the hospital? We'd run. We'd be the ambulance. We'd get them to safety. We'd be their salvation.

It only took a dozen or so trips for this adrenaline to fade. Another close call, another unnecessary death, another life-threatening situation. Near-death, experiences were becoming commonplace. Before coming to Malawi I had never seen a dead body, now I was carting them in my car. These were not nameless faces, these were my friends, these were people I knew. These were stories that I was now a part of.

The crudeness of death was what affected me the most. Death from unattended HIV/Aids, malaria that didn't get treated in time, malnutrition, death in childbirth, death from a septic graze that hadn't been treated with medicine, the death of a child falling from a mango tree. I was overwhelmed, I was out of my league, yet I was the one to be called to the rescue or I was the one to be blamed.

You can't live long term under these conditions, something in you snaps. Crying was a common practice in my life. It had to be if I were to survive living here. A funeral once a week for someone I knew. Another death threat, had become apart of my routine, but does that now make such things normal? It was so common that I feared it was my new normal. Was my life so fragile? Was death my new friend?

Normal is all about perspective. If it happens often enough, it then becomes 'normal', but not necessarily right, not necessarily fair or humane. The rawness of this kind of life would be an outrage where I come from in Australia. I had never known such pain, such suffering could still be happening in the world because I had never seen it, never experienced it. My ignorance was bliss. The bubble burst and my new reality was a rude awakening. To get my head around this, I'd draw on history, what I'd learnt about concentration camps, the depression, the Holocaust, stories of horrible suffering, neglect and needless death.

Simple operations conducted without anesthetic, nurses were too lazy to give medication. An apathy of hopelessness surrounded our local hospital. With eight wards and 380 beds for 1 400 000 people, on a good day, there'd be several doctors on duty as well as some clinical officers. Most medication disappeared before it got to patients. Where did it all go? I'd hear rumours of it being sold on the black market. It wasn't hard for me to relate what was happening before my very eyes to historical events.

Without God picking me up, dusting me off and giving me the courage I'd never make it. I'd reminded myself of his promises. He'd never put me through more than I could take, he'd never leave me. Only in his strength could I do this. It became my mantra. I'd remind him that it was he who'd called me. I was being obedient. This wasn't what I signed up for. It wasn't in the brochure, so he was going to have to do the impossible with my ordinariness.

When it was my turn to be hauled off to the hospital, we were no longer on the outside looking in. Tim found me unconscious on our bathroom floor, convulsing. Terror stood beside him holding his hand. Death was pushing its way into our own home? Like a fireman, he'd hauled me into the hospital desperate to find help. There was none. There was no medication for my suspected cerebral malaria. There was a small room with a vinyl-covered mattress. There was a bucket to clean up the mess I'd made. A dozen or so friends were crowding the room praying and hoping I would be alright, but there wasn't much hope.

Tim was forced to leave me with our teammate Robyn, an Australian Nurse who'd worked in the local hospital. She was on fire making a plan. Tim was to go to another clinic and get some medication. He had to make the minivan drive through the washed-out creek bed. He had to bribe the night guard to break into the medical stores. He had to pay off the medical staff to find the right medications. He had to do all this at 1am because my life hung in the balance.

We all like to say things like," I'd never do that!" But given the right circumstances, the perfect storm, I think we'd surprise ourselves. How far would you go, if it meant saving your wife's life? What would you do to rescue your kids? Our moral ground had been obliterated. What was common had now become normal for us. When Tim found me unconscious on the bathroom floor, we knew we could call international SOS to evacuate me to the nearby city and I would be flown to South Africa in a Lear jet. We knew I could be put in ICU with world-class machines monitoring my progress. I could be tested. I could see specialist doctors who would diagnose me and give me the right treatment. We knew I would most likely recover, I would have the best available to me so that I would make it through.

For the majority of the world population, this would never happen. For those living in Malawian villages, such concepts don't even exist in their vocabulary. It would take me six weeks before I could crawl the distance from my bed to our bathroom without resting intermittently. It would take months before I would feel like my old self again, but would I ever feel normal?

I've concluded that normal was what God first promised us when he put Adam and Eve in the garden of Eden. The mess we have made here on earth, the horrors we see around us were just common, not God's 'normal' plan for us at all. If I was to believe anything, I was to believe that my home was not here. My heavenly home was where I belonged. So until then, I was to accept my vulnerability. I was to work with this brokenness. I was to believe that in His strength, what didn't kill me made me stronger and I wasn't dead. He hadn't finished with me yet.

Chapter 43

HASSAN

Malawi

All the men had gone on leadership camp, except for one guy, Bilali who was chosen to stay around and look after the place and me. Bilali was like a big brother to me. He was the one I went to when I didn't know what to do. His patience and wisdom were incredible. I should have felt special that I need looking after, but sometimes it felt a little patronizing.

Tim had gone with the intent of teaching and workshopping more concepts of faith and salvation with the men in our community. Working out their faith with Godly fear. We knew it was going to be a spiritually 'hot' time. Some random event was bound to happen, come out of left field to test us and bring us to our knees.

The men left in the morning and I received a message in the afternoon. Hassan was in jail. Hassan a boy from our youth group who was a regular at our home; the kind of kid who always pushed the boundaries but had an endearing quality about him. He was naughty but really likable. His mother, a committed believer, worked hard as a sole parent to raise her family, but Hassan and his brother were too big for her to influence.

All young men are one day faced with a choice, to follow their friends or stand-alone and choose what is right. Hassan had chosen the former and was caught up with a local gang. We'd wondered why he hadn't been around for a while.

Apparently, he'd been caught up with some organized crime managed by two bosses not known locally. They rounded up potential teenagers looking for some action with the promise of wealth. Hassan had 'sucker' written all over his face. He'd been part of a set up to steal goats. One guy would distract the owner while the others would sneak in and take the goat. This time the owner got wise and caught one boy red-handed. No prizes for guessing who? Hassan wasn't savvy enough and was now in jail.

I went down to the police station with Hassan's mum, just to support her. It's not a good idea for me to show my face too much, to begin with. Westerners generally mean a higher bail price. Someone needed to go and work it all out, speak on the boy's behalf. It had to be a man but Hassan's uncle lived in another town and nobody had seen his father in years.

God always knows what he is doing. Bilali advised me to stay put as he prepared himself to mediate. We all prayed together and sent him off. Hassan had been roughed up a bit and tazered in private places trying to get a confession out of him. Even this wasn't enough for him to rat on the bosses. His life would be in danger if he did.

The first police officer Bilali saw happened to be a friend of his. God's favour had already begun. He'd look out for Hassan. After a bit of negotiating Hassan was allowed bail. However, he was to show up in court if the owner wouldn't drop the charges.

Later that day I went again with Hassan's mum to give him food. As I sat outside the police station I greeted and began chatting with a lady. It turns out she was the local magistrate for minors. A lovely lady who assured me that Hassan would be released. We sent bail the next day and he planted himself in our front yard. Shattered and humbled he wanted to assure me that he'd learnt his lesson. He wasn't going back to the gang. We prayed with him and warned him that the miracles he saw might not happen again if he deliberately went back.

Hassan hasn't been back to his gang, he stays home with his Mum and spends time talking with the old man who lives next door. He is still a loudmouth and often obnoxious but he has remained true to his promise. One day he came to tell me, he'd finished making some bricks. I'd agreed to help him with a roof if he made the bricks for a small hut. He wanted to give back to his Mum, so building a house would provide rent, a monthly income.

Sometimes we have to hit bottom before we learn our life lessons. Aren't we all slow learners? If only we would be quicker to listen and slower to act. Only by the grace of God do any of us stand.

Chapter 44

CHOOSING LIFE

Malawi

Life is really hard. Especially if you are a Yawo teenage boy who is trying to break the mould and get through school, do the right thing by your relatives and your religion. It is an impossible task, and our good friend Atupele had had enough. His mum called in a stage of panic. He'd gone. She had woken this morning and found a note on his bed. They had checked the river but perhaps they were too late. The entire extended family were out searching. The previous week the neighbour's son did the same thing and they found him drowned in the river two days later. Please, God, don't let this happen to Atupele. We prayed and searched and prayed again. No one had seen him since yesterday when he had a fight with his parents about coming home late.

Teenage boys have lots of energy and very few tools to deal with the life they are encountering, especially in the village. Atupele was 15 and hadn't yet chosen a girlfriend or had a child. Which is unusual for our community where fertility was prized. He had decided to follow Jesus and learned about faith at the kids' group where we taught God's word. He'd stopped coming since he was now older. He went to church with his Mum and the mosque with this Uncle. He was trying to stay in school. He was trying but felt like a failure.

Hours went by and still no word, no sign, nothing. We had searched everywhere. 'God you know where he is and what he needs to hear, please speak to him.'

At 2 pm in the afternoon that is exactly what God did. He spoke to Atupele in a clear audible voice. Instead of losing his life in the river, he went to the mountain to pray. He found life and new strength for living. God met him on the road and so he came home.

This story nearly broke my heart. I had two teenage boys who live in the village. Were they really any different? No, they weren't. We'd known Atupele since he was 5 years old. He played in our yard on most days. His family were our close friends. What could I do to help him and all the other teenagers we knew and loved? There is nothing for them in the village.

So we started a Yawo Youth Group (Not quite like the one at your church). God had made it clear to me these kids needed more. They needed to hear God's word that was real for them. Life lessons taught before the dramas unfolded. They needed a close group of friends who looked out for each other, and role models who set the standard of what a Yawo follower of Jesus looked like.

Yawo Youth Group has over 40 teenagers who come once a month. It is invitation only, selected kids who are serious about life and want to make a difference, our own sons included. God was raising up for himself a people, a new generation who were willing to make the right choices and stand.

Chapter 45

CONCERNS

Malawi

It had worried us that many of the local kids the boys played with were sexually active. Some already with children. The Yawo culture is different from our western worldview. Fertility was prized and the children who went through initiation ceremonies at a young age were taught to reproduce. It was taught as a gift and an important part of life. Most children in the village had experienced sex young. Girls often returned from initiation camps with the light of innocence gone from their eyes. We grieved this and prayed for ways to help. Such things reminded us of why we were here.

Our boys, budding teenagers, were easily old enough to become sexually active in Yawo culture, with lots of willing girls happy to help. We asked God for a way through this.

Jarred and Clayton studied through Education Queensland's Distance Education program in Malawi. Australia's State School System sent us to work to complete and we returned it throughout the year. The boys got Australian school report cards, they had teachers accessible via email. Our family valued education and spent a lot of time together in the classroom.

Around 16% of children in the region completed primary school. Education was not valued, as we valued it. It was seen as a peripheral part of life, something to do when the important was finished. However, God was making a change and he was using us to do it.

We have been watched. Our lives were lived in a fishbowl. How I dressed, how I stood, the look on my face, how I'd cut my tomatoes, when I'd take a shower was all known. Living in this community was like that. It had taken me years to get used to this. So our going to school every day and working together had been watched. Jarred and Clayton had been watched. The way they had grown up in the Yawo community had been watched. They were owned by the local people we knew and love. We didn't fit in here but we belonged. We were part of the furniture so to speak, a bit weird and very different, but loved just the same.

Those watching us had begun to mimic us. As much as this made me cringe, our lives were copied. Isn't copying someone a form of flattery? Because we valued education, education was becoming valued in the community. The children Jarred and Clayton had grown up with were staying in school. They brought us their report cards. They'd shown us the English they were learning. They invited us to school celebrations. If anything good happened at school, parents sent their kids to 'Mama' (yes, that's me) to show her.

With this wind of change happening right under or noses, we had seen a slow shift in cultural behaviour. Not that it happened because of us, but God was using us to make it happen.

Jarred and Clayton's friends were staying in school, a few of them had left, but many of them had seen another way, a new narrative. We treasured what was happening, the hope we saw in these kids as they actually planned for a brighter future. God had not only answered our prayers and protected our boys, but he had also moved a miracle in the community. Despite the fact that many of the boys' friends were sexually active, God had opened a door and given enough protection and wisdom to keep our sons safe. What a generous God we serve!

Chapter 46
FASTING

Malawi

Just so you know, fasting is really difficult for me. I feel like I need to confess, perhaps not to you, but to those who we live near. It is Ramadan and everyone is fasting, breakfast before dawn, then no food or water until evening. Everyone has empty stomachs and bad breath. Tim is fasting again this year too, to be in the battle against the lies and the spiritual oppression that comes with this time of year.

I have officially decided that I cannot do the Islamic style fast. Not drinking water is hard combined with no food just makes me feel way too dizzy to function. I could do it if I lay in bed all day, but that isn't really an option. It makes me feel more compassion for my friends in the village. They are working so hard in an attempt to ensure their place in eternity. If I felt dizzy, how much more so them? They still needed to feed their families and cart water and get up while it's still dark to cook porridge and collect firewood. Secretly I knew many women who cheated. They'd say they are fasting but they weren't. Some who were missing days now would try to make them up later in the year as they felt guilty for their weakness. They feared losing favour with God and felt guilty for not meeting the standards of the law.

I am still fasting, but not the same as the others. I want to hear God more. I want to be a part of the fight for freedom and salvation. But that is just it, I'm not following the law to win my salvation. It has been given to me as a free gift. My fast is a prayer that this free gift will be made known to the entire Yawo community. I pray that one day everyone would have the opportunity to hear the good news explained to them in a way they can understand, in a way that helps them make a choice.

Chapter 47

TAKING ACTION

Malawi

Tim had been teaching in the villages about being doers of the word and not hearers only. Hearing God's word was good but without action it was useless. We were often convicted by this in our own lives as we learnt to trust and take steps of faith.

The group of ladies at one village, in particular, took this to heart in a big way. At the end of the study on Matthew 5 about keeping anger in our hearts, unforgiveness and thinking bad thoughts there was a strong response. Half of the group came to the front, got on their knees and repented in prayer. They confessed how they had been harbouring angry thoughts against people who had wronged them. I sat encouraged by these ladies, encouraged and convicted.

I shuffled up the front amongst them and lay my forehead in the dust. "Forgive us our sins as we forgive those who have sinned against us." These words hurt my heart. I really didn't want to do this, but the fear of God not forgiving me was far greater than the hurt I wanted to hold on to. I could feel the Spirit's presence. Literally working in the hearts of those willing to take the step of faith and live the word not, just hear it.

This was not the first time I had to forgive those who had hurt me, I was to forgive them again and again and again. As often as the pain reminded me of my wounds, I was to forgive again and bless them.

You see, I've discovered this secret when it comes to wounds. The evil one wants to remind us of our pain, our wounds and our past. He feeds us lies that grip us in a state of bitterness and misery. But God has come to give us life and life to the full. As I forgave, God didn't forget, he would take care of those who have caused me harm. My forgiveness brought me freedom. It brought joy back to my life. There was no hold or heaviness over me, because this forgiveness healed my wounds, reminded me how loved I was and broke the chains that bound me.

Chapter 48

BEING TOO BUSY IS VANITY!

Australia and Malawi

My devotions screamed out at me. Being too busy is vanity! Is it really? Come on God, be nice to me, not only do I struggle with bitterness, now you're telling me I'm vain. Of course, he was right. But who likes being convicted?

I am too busy because I am vain. I want to appear important. Significant. What better way than to be busy? The incredible hours, the crowded schedule, and the heavy demands of my time were proof to myself and to all who would notice- that I was important. If I went into a doctor's office and found there was no one waiting, and I saw through a half-opened door the doctor reading a book, I would wonder if he was any good….

Such experiences affected me. I come from a society in which crowded schedules and harassed conditions were evidence of importance, so I developed a crowded schedule and harassed conditions. When others noticed, they acknowledged my significance, and my vanity was fed.

Eugene Peterson said it, but God delivered this truth slap to me. How do we slow down and let God be God and we be the servants he wanted us to be? I needed to let him lead and I was to follow. Spending time in the Word, praying. I'd established a routine of Spiritual Retreats, time to get away from the demands on my time and hide for a while. I likened it to a scene from the Narnia movies. In the middle of the battle, Lucy rode through the danger to find

Aslan. He defended her, he protected her and then sat calmly with her and asked, "Why didn't you come to me earlier." Spoiler alert! He then went and won the battle!

    Would you know, time is nothing for God. He can move mountains, make the sunrise and give or take away my very life in one heartbeat. Spending time with him, it was the only way to win the battle.

Chapter 49
LISTENING

Malawi

The Men's camp was happening in a few days. We were filled with expectation as we had just returned from home assignment. The men leading the village groups were gathering to prepare for the following months of teaching God's word. Our consultant, Roger was in the car with Tim, having just flown in to attend the training.

The road was littered with life. People buying and selling, others just wandering through, the markets are always like this, noisy, crowded and messy like a sideshow alley on a busy day. Tim crawled the car through the mud brushing past bikes and avoiding bodies, potholes and buckets of produce. Everyone got to share the road. In the middle of his conversation, Roger told Tim to stop the car. A quiet chill running down his spine, the engine was silent as he opened his door. The crowd had focused their attention. It was a miracle unfolding.

Under his back tyre lay a toddler. Their legs centimetres from the wheel. Some men began to shake the car shouting at Tim, blaming him for hurting the child. Tim's answer was lost in the noise. Out of the crowd, a familiar voice was heard. Mama Adija had worked with us for many years, she had been selling tomatoes nearby. Pushing through the crowd she grabbed the child showing everyone that it was fine.

Two men and the baby got in the car and Tim drove out of the mess off to the hospital. Crying but without a scratch the baby was unhurt. Tim found the

LISTENING

mother of the child 100 metres from the markets. The toddler had wandered off in the crowd unnoticed. She reassured Tim that he wasn't at fault and expressed how grateful she was for his diligence. In the busyness, they were able to hear that still quiet voice. By listening to the prompting, the life of a child was saved.

This story humbled me, how many times had I not listened? How many opportunities had gone by without me noticing?

Chapter 50

DISGUST

Malawi

Just next to our schoolroom, just metres away, there was an empty hut with a brick fence.

One day we were disturbed by a child screaming uncontrollably. So much so that we stopped school and went to investigate. Noise was normal in our community but this was way over the top. August was Initiation season, children in all the Yawo villages underwent a traditional ceremony that took several weeks to transform children into Yawo men and women.

This special ceremony was happening right next door to us in the empty hut. Six little boys ranging from 6-10 years were becoming men, through circumcision and ceremony. It was unusual to have it happen so close in town, but understandable if there was nowhere else to meet. Upon our investigation, my heartstrings were thrown into a knot of controversy. They had a two-year-old in there, being initiated! The child didn't know what was going on and was terrified.

Standing only metres away not being able to see we heard the child's suffering and cries for his mother. He cried all day. I spend hours praying, " Lord what should I do? This was none of my business but I could not stand by and do nothing while the child suffered so."

Eventually, it was too much for me, and I let it be known that I was concerned for the child. When was cultural sensitivity necessary and when is it time to step in and make a fuss? Well, fuss I did (in a culturally appropriate way) and

DISGUST

the child was taken to its mother after a few days, leaving the ceremony early. Following my heart God gave me reassurance for my actions when the story got out into the community, most were expressing their disgust at the inappropriateness of it all. It wasn't culturally right that a two-year-old child should be taken from their mother to be initiated. Traditions were changing and carelessness and cruelty can slip by unnoticed if we don't speak out.

Chapter 51

STRENGTH

Malawi was in a small hut, the room packed with local ladies. There was enough space for each one to sit on the floor, but there was room for little else. Toddlers wandered in and out of the open door. The lucky ones got a wall to lean on while the rest adjusted themselves to find a little more comfort. It was a light and airy morning filled with a sense of expectation. This was not a funeral, this was a time of celebration.

We had come to hear God's word. There were about 30 of us in that space, from villages all over. Twelve different villages in all represented. The women were known as leaders in their community. I sat amongst them. They were mostly my elders, grandmothers with years of experience leading to the wisdom of life.

Women like this don't have time to waste. They don't worry about what image they are portraying. They haven't got a word to say about the superficial things of life. They are serious about what matters. They are serious about what makes a difference. We listened to the word of God. What does a group of followers of Jesus look like? What does a leader need to do? The fear of God was the key to wisdom. Faith, hope and love. Without love, we could do nothing. What did love look like in a Yawo village? Carrying water for your sick neighbour? Sharing your food when they were hungry? Showing kindness when everyone else was being harsh?

There was joy in the room, the ladies burst into song, dancing and singing. These words were life and light to us. We needed this to stay strong. Could we stay strong? Could we live a life contrary to our traditions? Would we be different? The message would echo for days. I could sense the Holy Spirit moving. It was my turn to speak. I was the only foreigner there, but I was not a stranger. I knew these ladies and they knew me. "Listen to Mama", they told the new ones. She speaks Ciyawo. She teaches God's word. I was honoured and humbled by their respect, full of joy because I now belonged. I quietly prayed for God to give me the right words to share. These ladies were my sisters, deep Yawo women who were working out their faith. "Allahu Akbar" is spoken out in agreement. God is good.

There is so much more to faith than what is on the surface. I saw Jesus working in the lives of these ladies. It made me wonder what else would I still need to change? What else was I holding onto, in a feeble attempt to remain in control? Was I practising what I was preaching?

My journey had come the full circle, from the stranger to the host. I was not Yawo but I didn't have to be. I needed to be me. I needed to be all God created me to be. I sat in that confidence. I sat in that truth. *'He who had called me was faithful and he would do it!"* 1 Thessalonians 5:24

Finishing when the cool of the afternoon settled, while we were packing up, a message came through. On the way to the meetings, someone stopped to give a lift to a woman. They were heading in that direction anyway, a simple gesture that happened all the time. The driver was deep in conversation in the cab of the vehicle and forgot to stop to let the woman out. The woman was filled with terror, so much so that she jumped out of the moving vehicle. Her head hit the bitumen and her body went limp. The vehicle had driven on, the driver unaware of what had just happened.

It was reported that the woman wrongly assumed she was being kidnapped. (Taken to be sold at the border into Mozambique.) Despite what the other ladies in the car had said to reassure her, she was filled with terror. Rumours had become a reality in her mind. She risked her life to flee because a lie had grown bigger than the truth. With a fractured skull, she had been admitted into the hospital. They didn't know if she would make it. The room went silent as we bowed our heads in prayer.

    This was what happened to those without Jesus, fear consumed and decisions were made without reason. We were spurred on to share the good news back in our home villages. I was spurred on to remain here and cherish what God had called me to do. I was spurred on to break through such fear, to tell the truth, and speak the freedom we could have if we chose to trust. It was the perfect lesson to hold me steady and stay on that narrow path.

Chapter 52

~~~

WHAT I DON'T KNOW

Malawi

It was teacher training day, the one day a year of training for all those who volunteered to teach the children in their villages, God's word, bible stories. Life-changing stories that happened to other people thousands of years ago, but made sense and applied to everyday life now.

I welcomed everyone in the traditional Yawo manner and began the day by asking one of the male leaders to pray. He stood, opened his hands and spoke in Arabic, a prayer that he has recited since he was a child but spoke now with new meaning because of his faith. *'God you are good and you care for us. We invite you today to show us the way, to teach us and give us your peace.'*

Each person stood in turn and explained who they were and where they were from. Yawo would do this by saying where they lived and contrast it to where they were born. For example in English, I am Melanie, I live in Karonga village but my family comes from Australia. Identity is important.

We didn't all know each other, so this was a good way to place people, who they were and where they belonged. We then opened God's word and read two stories. One from Mark 4: 30-32 The Kingdom of God is like a mustard seed, and Mark 10:13-16, Jesus says to let the little children come to me. We talked about our faith beginning as a little seed but it grew into a mighty tree. Allowing our kids the opportunity to grow up knowing a God who loved them. It was a mind-blowing idea.

I looked around and saw so many faces, so many stories of what God was doing. First-generation believers were blazing a trail in their own villages. Not without hardship and opposition but they were children of the King so they held their heads high and trusted the one who rescued them from hopelessness.

We broke into groups to answer three questions each. When did you meet Jesus? Where did you meet Jesus? Who told you about him?

I had no idea the incredible stories that would come from such simple questions. I wished I could have recorded them all.

So few had an opportunity to learn anything when they were young, they explained that they either went to church or the mosque and sometimes both, but learnt a lot of rituals without understanding the meaning. Most met Jesus when they were adults, most had come to faith in the last 10 years. Most had heard about Jesus because Tim and I told someone, and someone told them the good news.

It wasn't supposed to include Tim and I, it was supposed to be about these new believers. But this day we got a glimpse of what happened if you were obedient and available. Bumbling our way through, Tim and I were misty-eyed and melted into the shadows as each one stood and shared their story.

I will tell you two of these stories.

One young mum stood up last in her group. She'd been waiting the whole time and I felt bad for her. I didn't know her at all, I had only met her an hour ago, I didn't want to make her uncomfortable and waited on the side ready to step in if she needed me to. She didn't. She introduced herself and began to explain that she was one of 4 children. When she was young, her brothers and sister died one by one from various sicknesses. Then when she was a bit older, her Mum died, then her Dad. She was left on her own.

Moving to her Aunty's house in a different village she met one of our leaders from the village groups. He invited her along to hear God's word, to hear about Jesus. She listened, she believed, she stood there strongly in front of everyone and told them. "My life began full of death, but now that I know the truth, I have life and I can give that life to not only my children but other children in the village;

a life of hope in a God who loves them. I now volunteer each week to teach the children God's word. " Then she quietly sat down.

The second story was from a lady I knew very well. Well, a lady whom I saw almost every day but clearly I didn't know everything about her. She told her story in the group that was on the other side of the maize field. Too far away from where I was. I only heard it second hand as the group leader gave the summary.

Mama S lived on the other side of the airstrip (the airstrip that has never had any actual aircraft ever land on it and is now full of houses, but everyone still called it the airstrip.) She met someone who knew someone who sent their kids to the kids club in our compound to play with Jarred and Clayton. Her kids came home with stories of God. They came home different. So different that she began to ask more questions. She wasn't satisfied with what she found out so she plucked up the courage to meet one of the other mums.

She asked if she could come and join us. That was over six years ago now.

'She's now a strong member of the ladies group and teaches in the kids club. She is now a woman of faith that remains strong in her religious identity but knows for sure where her hope comes from. There's only one way to God and that's through Jesus.' She was now earning a wage through the nursery school that the group runs and contributes a tithe from the profits of this business to the running of kids clubs in other villages.

So, see how the kingdom of God is literally like a mustard seed. Something tiny can grow into something huge that spreads its branches wide, far wider than we had ever expected!

Chapter 53

DREAMING BIG

Malawi

It all started with three of us, two local ladies and myself. I'd met these ladies in my first weeks in Malawi and we decided that we were going to be friends. Sometimes you just know that you're going to click with someone. We planned to meet each week and pray together. They were women of such faith, little did I know how much I would learn from this relationship. It was going to change my life.

We made a list of things to pray for, life-changing things. We committed to this list daily and without ceasing. We prayed throughout the night, we fasted, we chanted, we danced, we cried and laughed, we proclaimed, we begged, we waited.

It didn't take long before things were getting crossed off this list and others added. Seeing answers to prayers was a buzz. We loved the tangible presence of a God who was listening to us. As I visited other local ladies throughout the week, they asked me to pray with them too. A story of answered prayer is the best inspiration to bring your own requests to God.

The ladies group began from these humble beginnings, meeting together, praying and living side by side. Our kids were young and would play around us while we studied God's word, claimed his promises and did our best to obey his commands.

Each week the regular ladies would come and bring friends, over the years there must be more than 100 ladies who have come and gone from this group. Groups are like that, dynamic as people come and go in and out of our lives.

The core group stayed, by now we've been meeting together for nearly 10 years. We've studied God's word every week and worked through a dozen programs. The group of ladies had transferred their enthusiasm to their own children. A few of us joined together with our kids to teach them bible stories. With the few growing now to well over 300 attending regularly in our compound, with sister groups spreading to other villages. They came to hear God's word taught in their own language. We kept it simple; play games, sing songs and teach a bible story. Kids from the community hearing about an opportunity to learn without strings attached. The group grew from my friend's kids to her friend's kids, then to her friend's friends' kids and so on.

These kids' groups have now become an institution in the community, they run easily without me driving it, it is about love, acceptance and belonging. The ladies group had learned to trust each other in a community where trust was scarce. They were reliable and diligent, keeping their promises to God and each other. It was beautiful to belong, to be part of something bigger than yourself, something that didn't happen because of you but wouldn't have happened without you if you know what I mean.

One day these ladies started dreaming. I love it when I hear their heart. Sometimes ladies in the village can get bored. They cart water, they tend their farms, they cook food, they go to the market, they chat with friends, maybe buy and sell in small business, look after their family. Not much changes, routines can get boring, topics of discussion can get dull, refusing gossip becomes harder. Perhaps we can do more with our lives?

We'd been discussing this for a long time and tried all sorts of ways of doing things differently. I have to admit, I was feeling the monotony myself. Nothing was wrong with my life but I was ready for a challenge, something different, new and interesting.

So we prayed and talked, and prayed some more. Then an idea dawned on us that fit. Perhaps you know what this is like? Something in your heart gels with the fit. It resonates; it just makes sense but at the same time scares you silly with possibilities of success and failure. Were we willing to take the risk?

'Well God if you're in this then make it stick to all of us.' We put out our fleece. It was not a rash decision, it was calculated, it was measured. It was a year later, after looking into all the options and risks, doing reconnaissance, research and surveys, getting the right ticks in the right boxes.

Then we were ready. *CC Daycare and Nursery school* was opened. A group of Mums with young kids, looking after a group of kids of young Mums in the local community. It was a business venture with such promise. It's a cash crop, an income-generating venture to fund local faith community projects and programs. Women who were willing to try something out of their comfort zone and limited opportunity, who were committed to each other, willing to take a risk and trust that God would do the rest. Ordinary ladies without a fancy formal education, who are willing to be trained and stretched so that they could make their lives better for themselves and those around them.

The critics were waiting on the sideline ready to issue their judgment. To shut us down and say I told you so. It's hard when you're already struggling in confidence to hear the ridicule as you pass by. No matter how people treat you, never forget you are a daughter of the King. Hold your head high, and take one day at a time. Small steps each day can take you a long way.

So the program's not perfect, there are problems that keep coming, there's conflict within the group. Money issues bring out the best and worst in all of us. The learning curve is steep, but we've been operating successfully. The business belongs to us, a committee of which I'm a part of, we have a history together. No one owns us, no one is the boss, we share the load with each one working in their areas of strength; carers, teachers, cleaners, treasurer, secretary, management, promotion and so on. With each one doing their part so that the whole group benefits. You might have heard of this model before? I believe it's found in 1 Corinthians 12:12.

Pioneering is difficult, but the trail blazed leads to opportunities beyond our control. Sustainable ministry, independence and interdependence in community, future security and growth, industry and education. Trust, commitment, reliability, forward planning, self-control, diligence, cooperation, dignity, resilience, persistence, patience, kindness, goodness, faithfulness, hope and love.

Chapter 54

JUMPING AGAIN

Into the unknown

So now you can see that jumping has become part of who I am and I don't want to live life without it. A life without trust, risk and failure is no life at all. Living safely can so easily become boring, boring becomes apathy and apathy, meaninglessness, depression, heartache and hopelessness. I want to live a life that matters, a life with purpose and passion.

God came to rescue us from a life of meaninglessness, the emptiness that comes when you are not challenged, not stretched, not growing. God's kindness is off the charts, he never pushes us harder than we can cope with, but he pushes us where we need to go. Sometimes that is a place of hurt, but in the long run, it grows us and makes us stronger and healthier.

The process of sanctification, the refining of our souls is a gift. It should make us feel loved and cherished, the time and precision God gives to our learning is an expression of his love.

Jumping into the unknown isn't recklessness nor is it immaturity or ignorance. It is deeply personal obedience. God speaks to each of us individually, everyone's story is different. Everyone's style is unique. How, when and where you jump is completely between you and God. We need to jump off the foundation of his word, we need to know it's truth. We will all stand before him face to face one day to give an account of our obedience.

How liberating is that? I'm only accountable for my actions, and you for yours. We don't need to carry the weight of the world on our shoulders. We don't need to live in a state of worry or fear. God holds us, he protects and guards us intimately, he doesn't make mistakes and he doesn't create nasty situations to punish us. This broken world and the evil around us is not his doing. He certainly is in control but he allows us to make our own decisions, make our own mistakes. He painfully watches us reject him, he grieves at the mess we've made and he waits patiently for us to surrender to his plans. His good, good plans!

Our story is not finished yet, as we face the future. We are to jump not knowing what is in store. Again we'll have to learn a new normal, what is common is not normal for us. Yet again we will be out of our league, overwhelmed by the new, a new way of living, it seems we aren't to get too comfortable.

What we do in private influences who we are in public. You don't have to go to Africa to jump. Our thought lives, secrets, dependencies and attitudes can cripple us where we stand. The stories I've shared with you have been shared to inspire and motivate you to hear God's voice, make changes, address the issues you're facing in life. To hear God correctly we need to know the Bible, we need to listen to the Holy Spirit in our soul and we need to be particularly aware of how the circumstances of our lives are arranged. With God there are no mistakes or coincidences, there is just one incredible story, one perfect plan, all he requires from us is to hold his hand and jump!

Jumping Inspiration

"No eye has seen, no ear has heard, no mind conceived what God has prepared for those who love him" but God has revealed it to us by his Spirit. The Spirit searches all things, even the deep things of God. **1 Corinthians 2: 9-10 NIV**

The greatest glory in living life is not in never falling, but in rising every time we fall. **Nelson Mandela**

So be strong and courageous. Do not be afraid and do not panic before them. For the Lord, your God will personally go ahead of you. He will neither fail you nor abandon you. **Deuteronomy 31:6**

Twenty years from now you will be more disappointed by the things that you didn't do than by the ones you did do. So throw off the bowlines, sail away from the safe harbour. Catch the trade winds in your sails. Explore, Dream, Discover. **Mark Twain**

Change is the essence of life. Be willing to surrender what you are for what you could become. **Anonymous**

God will not necessarily protect us – not from anything it takes to make us like His Son. A lot of hammering and chiselling and purifying by fire will have to go into the process. **Elizabeth Elliot**

It is a fearful thing to fall into the hands of the living God.... Therefore do not cast away your confidence, which has great reward. For you have need of endurance, so that after you have done the will of God, you may receive the promise. **Hebrews 10: 31, 35-36**

Our lives begin to end the day we become silent about things that matter. **Martin Luther King Jnr**

When one door closes, another opens; but we often look so long and so regretfully upon the closed door that we do not see the one which has opened for us. **Alexander Graham Bell**

I have always been delighted at the prospect of a new day, a fresh try. One more start with perhaps a bit of magic waiting somewhere behind the morning. **Joseph Priestley**

God knows all hearts, and he sees you. He will keep watch over your soul. **Proverbs 24:12**

We crucify ourselves between two thieves: regret for yesterday and fear of tomorrow. **Fulton Oursler**

Our greatest fear as individuals should not be of failure but of succeeding at things that don't really matter. **Tim Kizziar**

Encore

BONUS STORIES

ON A LIGHTER NOTE

Malawi

It's not nice to finish on a heavy note, so I'll tell you something more lighthearted. It is very healthy to be able to laugh at yourself. Or even better to laugh at or even better with your husband!

It was dark and Tim had just driven in, home from his day in the village. All I could see was his back as he held open the car doors and tossed things out over his shoulder rather frantically.

'Hi, welcome home. What on earth are you doing?" said me, his sweetly supportive wife.

He swung around, "Don't come near me!"

"What? Why?"

"There's infectious disease everywhere in the car!"

He had picked up this unconscious woman, covered in shingles and disease. He'd taken her to the clinic and then the hospital. He'd saved her life but was now set on killing the enemy in the car!

An hour and nearly a whole bottle of disinfectant later, the car was spotless and disease-free. Then he went on to disinfect himself.

We went inside for dinner and in an attempt to lighten his mood, I suggested we watch a DVD. We're up to series 2 of Hawaii 5 O. It's what we super-spiritual people do to wind down after an interesting day!

Guess what the story was about?

A guy with a strange infectious disease! Ha!

THIS IS FUNNY HONEY.

Malawi

This is funny honey, and I blame Uncle Laurie, Jeff and Al, Hodgy and Karl all of whom encouraged my husband to attempt such things. I am referring to beekeeping. I don't know if it is called anything else fancier but at least you know what I am talking about.

Tim decided to try beekeeping so built a hive here in Malawi, followed the internet instructions and put together one of those white boxes full of frames, one on top of the other. It looked really good and all was going well. That is until we got to our first problem, a slight oversight on our behalf. How does one get a swarm of bees in the hive?

We located a natural hive in our friend's roof and it moved (well actually you don't say moved you say 'swarmed' it's a bee term) a few days later into the top of the tank stand. So we put the hive underneath, opened the lid and waited. Nothing happened.

So we smeared it with honey and added water bowls. Nothing happened.

Plan B. Malawians have solutions for all sorts of problems. Hence enter the Bee Man; a local guy, rough-looking, smoking like a chimney (and who would blame him for what he was about to do) out of the village wearing a singlet, shorts and thongs. He lights a fire underneath the ladder and then climbs the ladder, and grabs the entire hive with his bare hands.

Thousands of bees raging mad stinging him everywhere! Smoke so thick we thought he was going to pass out. Apparently not, apparently, he does this sort of thing all the time!

Surprised he's not dead!

Anyway, so then he had a swarm in the hive. Enter another beekeeping phenomenon, bees can swarm and just move if they don't like where they are. Obviously, Tim's nice white house didn't cut it in terms of bee luxury, so they moved out and settled under our front verandah! Now, what do we do? So we called the Bee Man back from the village, smoke and all. Then we got clever after that and locked them in the hive. Well, you don't lock them as such, just block off the entrance with a piece of wood.

We read a bit more helpful information on the internet and after a while, our bees settled down and we unblocked the entrance. They then got on with their lives and started gathering honey! Happy Bees! Yay!

O.K. so then comes the well-known stage of raiding the hive for honey. We found a few problems with this. Firstly, most of our local friends are terrified of bees, so Tim resorted to getting our Malawian workers to give him a hand. All extremely interested in getting honey, not many really liking being in close proximity to the hive though. (There could be some moral issues here because this was way above their pay grade.)

Tim began problem-solving and went to the local tailor. He cut up mosquito nets and bought local straw hats. We made our own bee suits, hats and nets, tucked into overalls with socks and shoes and gloves. Not only did these outfits look attractive, but they were also very functional! (Actually, they looked ridiculous!)

Everyone waited until the cover of darkness before the raid began. Sounds exciting hey! Six men all kitted out, smoke billowing everywhere, so much so that no one could really see what they were doing. They sneak in and open the hive. It is full of honey. Our first Malawian friend brings over the burning torch he is holding and begins to set the hive alight. 'Stop, Stop, we don't want to burn the hive we just take the honey out!' Obviously, there are cultural differences in

Bee Keeping. Malawians don't reuse hives; a raid is a one-off deal. Burn the lot and get the honey. Tim lost a few of his helpers as a result of this new insight.

They got the frames out and fled the site. Back over beside the fire, they began to get the honey off the frames. Grown men usually have an element of decorum when it comes to doing the tough stuff. But not so much when it comes to raiding a beehive. We saw guys running in circles, putting their hands and feet in fires and screaming like little kids, with lots of wild arm flapping and dancing about. Really fun to watch from a distance! The honey was fantastic and so everyone got stuck into it, eating the comb and all. Such a frenzy that a few ended up with stings on their tongues, lips and face.

We'd been doing this for about 18months, getting a steady supply of our own honey and Tim growing a healthy respect for bees in the process. Then we met our friend Charles. Charles is a French Belgian guy, a businessman in Malawi. He knows about bees and he'd heard of our beekeeping attempts. I think he just felt plain sorry for us but through his contacts, we were able to purchase some real proper beekeeping suits!

Now we looked good! So good, in fact, that I was tempted to give it a try. We decided that Saturday afternoon was a good time. Most beekeeping folks raid the hive during the day in these proper suits so we thought we would do the same. We told the kids to keep away, Benny our day guard found something to do on the other side of the compound. We were set.

I felt like one of those people who appear after a nuclear disaster. Although there was no breathing apparatus I was walking kind of stiffly in the suit feeling rather heroic. We were about to show these bees real technology. We even had a proper smoker, not just a wad of sticks on fire. Such professionalism.

In we walked and opened up the hive. Tim with his new beekeeping frame remover lifted out the first frame. I smoked it a bit and we put it in the bucket. A few more bees came and started getting a bit angry at us, but our super suits were doing their job. More smoke, more frames. Easy! We walked out of the garden and back to the table. As we walked I noticed that nothing seemed to change much. There were as many bees following us as there were back at the hive. I walked on a bit further and they still followed. Not to be deterred we commenced removing the honey from the frames. More bees came, then more! This was not what was supposed to happen. The calm voice of my ever-adventurous husband was beginning to shake. (Remember he's terrified of bees) "Let's just take these remaining frames back to the hive, perhaps that will make them happy.' It didn't. I smoked that smoker, but it did nothing, we lit fires around the garden, it did nothing. We had some really angry bees and they were not leaving us no matter what we did.

I ran the honey into our yard and covered it up, perhaps that would settle them down. We went back to the hive to close it up only to discover that the bees had turned on the chickens we keep in the same garden. They were dying everywhere. Panicked, we began trying to save our chickens. Gloves full of honey, trying to light matches for the smoker, I choked and began swatting the bees off the half-dead chickens. It didn't work. Tim began picking up the now blind chickens and putting them in their cage. However chicken wire doesn't keep out bees, so it made no difference!

"Let's just chase them out of the yard." So Tim and I began to run about the garden chasing the already blind and half dead chickens, who weren't really running anywhere. It was easier for me to just walk over and pick them up. By then it was horrible to see the half-dead things flipping about. Tim began to give them a quick death, and then piled them up near the beehive. Thinking that maybe the carnage would satisfy the vengeance of the bees. (I'm not sure that bees really think like this.)

I've never really been the farming type, typically practical and capable, but not very experienced in the area of animal husbandry. So picture this situation if you may. Here I am the ever-supportive wife. Decked out in my super suit, covered in bees, chasing and picking up blind chickens in the 40 plus degree heat without a clue of what to do next. Then it hit me. Bees can't fly in the rain. (I'd watched the Bee movie with my kids and remembered this part.) So I ran home and got the hose shoving it over the fence.

Tim gave me a nod of approval. Good idea. We sprayed it everywhere. Trying to get the bees off the chickens. It didn't work, not only now did we have poor chickens covered in bees. We had poor, wet, chickens covered in bees! Not such a good idea. One rooster was so blind and desperate, I hosed it to get it to move, only to see it shelter under the beehive?! Stupid thing! We had a line of chickens, half-dead, outside the garden gate, as I had picked them up and 'rescued them'- they were easy to squirt with the hose. But it wasn't really making the bees leave. I thought they would fly away and leave us alone, but no, they can fly in the rain and they didn't leave!!

Tim appeared with a can of 'Doom' (Malawi's 'Baygon' insect spray). He doused the remaining chickens, who by this time had hundreds of stings over their body, so sad. With the fires burning out because of the hosing, and the air beginning to clear a bit, our situation calmed. Tim got some feed and water for the remaining chickens and we gathered around them saying a little prayer.

Our night guards were extremely happy about all this. Not only did they get some honey, but the dead chickens also provided meat for their meal that night. I also ensured everyone entering the compound that afternoon got an antihistamine, I was taking no chances and the night guards were delighted. Tim, however, was rather miffed about the whole situation, not really understanding why the bees got so angry. Perhaps it was the time of day? Perhaps we did something else wrong?

I am not really sure, but there was silence for a while. Experienced wives know that in the midst of a disaster one does not offer too many suggestions, ask questions or talk too much about things. One simply remains supportive. So we took off our super suits, killed a few more bees, iced our stings and strained the honey.

It wasn't until later that night Tim and I sat down together. Finally, he saw the funny side of the entire disaster. I asked what he wanted for dinner. Then came spontaneous laughter until our sides ached. Would you believe it, we answered together, "Honey chicken anyone?"

WONDERWOMAN FOR A DAY

Malawi

Not very often do I feel like a superhero. Mostly I get to feel very ordinary and am regularly reminded of what I can't do well. God is so completely generous with me (I think I'm one of his favourites just quietly) because out of left wing a door opened.

Many years ago we had a South African family live close by. They became our very good friends as we homeschooled our children together, prayed together and generally had fun together. Sadly they moved to the city (in Malawi but 3hrs drive away). We still got to see them but not as often. Fast forward seven years or so, the supermum of this family, Julie-Ann, now works as a Physical Education teacher at an International School. She's a great contact to have letting us know if there were any events on that us village people could come to the big smoke and join in.

She called us one day last year and asked if our boys would like to join their school swimming club as they needed high school swimmers. Without even asking my boys, this supermum signed them up. There was nothing else to do here anyway and opportunities like this come about once every blue moon. As a result of this, Jarred and Clayton competed in the Malawi National Swimming Competition. It was an incredible experience.

This year we signed up again. God had opened up another door for us. A local lodge near the lake had built a 39 metre lap pool 15 minutes from our house! (Yes, it is 39metres. Tim measured it with a measuring tape.) What were the odds of that! Despite it being literally in the middle of a paddock, and mostly so dark and murky that you'll bang your head on the end before you see it. We had a training pool!!

The first few training sessions didn't go to plan. Tim neared the end of the pool and was confronted with a black mamba (snake) that must have also been training! We realized that getting away from a snake very quickly wasn't something we needed to train for. Instincts kicked in and I watched Tim turn into an acrobat right before my very eyes.

We've also had frogs, grasshoppers (hundreds of them), very big beetles, frog eggs and some other strange slimy green stuff that I still don't what it is. But we are not deterred easily, our training began.

At the pre-National swimming gala (carnival but they call them galas here) my supermum friend asked me if I would like to join her and some other supermums in the Malawi Masters swimming team.

Not one to say no to a group of ladies offering me such an opportunity, I agreed. We were to swim at the Malawi Nationals and if our times were good enough, we could then go to Botswana to represent Malawi at the CANA International Championships.

Wow, wow, wow! How exciting, of course, I was in. I was already training in our super-duper lap pool. I could do this, couldn't I?

After the excitement settled down, I was confronted with the reality of two rather large obstacles. Firstly, you had to wear FINA approved swimwear (of which my board shorts and T-shirt were not). Secondly, you had to be able to turn, dive and generally not get disqualified because swimming has like a million rules when it comes to serious competition.

If you don't already know, I live in rural Malawi. Which means there are no swimwear shops to go to. We have a clothes market, bundles of clothes, second-hand rejects from overseas, that are laid out on the ground for us to rummage through. So I prayed and went looking. I have in the past found a Chinese Olympic tracksuit, and Italian cycle club jersey, an American Track and Field T-shirt, so finding a super swimming suit might not be that impossible.

Well after weeks of looking, I did find something. A triathlon, competitors suit with built-in padding for cycling and a zip upfront. A one-piece perfect if I was doing a triathlon. Close but not quite what I needed.

So not to be discouraged, I contacted another supermum, Michelle who lived in Australia and had kids who were seriously good swimmers. Perhaps she would know what to do? One thing I haven't mentioned… if you've never met me face to face, you wouldn't know that I am really tall. I'm 183 cm (6ft), which means that even when I lived in Queensland, I could never find a one-piece swimsuit that wouldn't cut me in half.

Well, Michelle, knew someone who knew someone and I'm not asking too many questions, because I think she might have had to go on the black market for such things. But a super-suit was found, Speedo brand and the proper longer leg version that covers up all sins. Praise God! It did make me laugh when she said she'd tried it on to see if it would fit me. Michelle is tiny, a foot shorter than me and weighs as much as my right leg! Anyway, I will never question her again, because the super suit fit like a glove! My Mum was coming to Malawi for Christmas, so I had the super-suit within the month!

The first hurdle sorted, miracle number one, now there was only the problem of learning the rules, how to turn and dive etc. Let me ask you a question? When was the last time you dove into a swimming pool? Well, for me it was when I was about twelve. Forty plus year old women don't dive into swimming pools even when they are swimming training with their sons! They just elegantly slide in, or perhaps on an energetic day, they jump in. I was way out of practice.

So, how many times do you think one has to dive into a pool to remember how to do it properly? How long does it take to forget bad habits and learn new ones when you're an old dog? The answer is much more and a lot longer than you'd first think. I thought I was diving like a pro but apparently, that was only in my head. My wonderful and completely honest family gently described my diving as more of a 'belly flop slash train wreck'. I was in trouble!! There is no advantage in being an International or even a National Masters swimming champion if you can't dive!

So I practiced and practiced and tried again. Not only do you have to be able to dive in without belly-flopping, but you have to dive in so that you're goggles don't fall off, fill up with water, fall down and cover your mouth or the worst of them all, stay on and fill up with water rendering you completely blind. Just to make matters worse, in butterfly, backstroke and breaststroke if anything happens to your goggles and you try to fix them whilst swimming, you will be disqualified.

I hope you noticed that I mentioned before that there are a million rules for swimming. I am proud to say that I could identify only about ten rules that were real obstacles for me. Not all that bad if I say so myself.

Tumble turns have never been a strong point in my swimming career. Although my swimming career consisted of competing in a carnival when I was in high school, then getting my bronze medallion and Ausswim ticket when I was teaching and competing in a few triathlons. I don't have much to show for competitive swimming prowess. It took me about a minute and 3 attempts at tumble turning to realize that it wasn't good time management to try to learn such a skill when I was to race in the nationals next month. So I spent time 'Googling' how to not get disqualified instead.

I should mention that there are only short course swimming pools in Malawi. 50m pools don't exist, and for us, spoilt Queenslanders who have one in every town, swimming a 50m race means you have to learn to turn and do it fast!

All this said I want to express how nervous I was after realizing that, how well I thought I could swim didn't match up with how well I could actually swim. My times, that were recorded in our 39m pool for the 50m, weren't that good! Admittedly it was hard to be exactly accurate when we would just put a chair at the 11-meter mark after I had done my turn and doubled back. Also, I refused to train backstroke anymore because of the injuries I'd sustained. You see, there were no lane ropes, no pretty flags showing you the end was near, nor was there anything to guide you when swimming. I could swim from one side of the pool to the other side then bang my head on the end whilst all the time thinking I was going straight!

So race day came. I had not been this nervous for a long time! I made sure that I looked like a parent coming to watch and not an old lady trying to swim. Watching our boys compete was a great distraction. They were in the early races and were smashing their PBs. (In swimming this means personal best times but no one says that only non- swimming people!) I was a super proud Mum, the boys from the village were holding their own!

All went well until it was my turn. I was standing up on the blocks, the loudspeaker announcing my name. "Melanie Downes lane 7." (I was either in lane 1 or 7 because I was the rookie with terrible times. Yes, that was a bit embarrassing, but not enough to stop me.) I was in a race at the Malawi Nationals. I was doing it. It was really happening, and I was wearing my super suit!

I must admit that I was so nervous for this first race that I forgot about everything. I didn't tighten up my goggles as I should have. I didn't pull down my swimming cap. When I dove in, the worst combination happened. Goggles full of water that stayed on. I had two perfectly round fish ponds strapped to my eyes rendering me blind. Now if you were a pro-swimmer like Michael Phelps you wouldn't be deterred and you'd just count your strokes and swim like you've done a million times before. Well, this was 50m breaststroke and I'd only ever trained in a 39-meter pool with a chair at the 11-meter mark. Counting my strokes wasn't going to do anything because I didn't know how many strokes it took for me to reach the end of the pool.

I was completely blind as I swam, so much so that when I did reach the end of the pool, it kind of snuck up on me. I hit the end without knowing it, disqualifying myself because you have to hit the end both hands above the water simultaneously! Fortunately, I managed to finish the race in some form of dignity with my supermum friend Julie-Ann in the lane next to me, full of delight and encouragement! I still had seven races left, hopefully, that was going to be my worst one.

In these moments of vulnerability in my life, God has always given me a silver lining. For me this was having my sons and Tim, right there cheering me on, as well as one of my best friends, Liz. She worked with us five years ago in a two-year internship here in Malawi. She had recently visited us, then landed a job with a Non-Government Organization in Lilongwe and had only moved to Malawi two months ago. I did wonder if God had completely turned her life around just so I could have a super fan at my debut? Maybe not, but that's what I told her and she relished the task at being a cheerleader for the entire carnival!!

After my disaster race, I was back on the blocks another seven times. Yes, seven times. I had only entered six races but the gala included team relays and they needed me to fill in. I will mention that I was considering making a new prize category for the Master Swimmer who could get over the lane ropes and get out of the pool before the other race began. Getting out of the pool is nearly impossible there were no steps or ladders. I looked like a seal on an iceberg!

Now that I've given you the raw truth, I need to finish on a high note. From eight races I came away with two golds and three silvers. Not bad for an old girl! Botswana here I come!!!

A NIGHT TALE

Malawi

There's a night guard who works with us, who was like a pillar in our lives. We love him, he is as solid as a rock, consistent and never changing, full of respect, diligent and always kind. (Yes we're rather fond of him.)

We have a story of when we first met him. Those were the days when we had to go to the schoolroom to watch a movie as there was no T.V. in our house. One night Tim and I must have watched something scary because when the movie finished it was later at night and we both erupted into a sprint back to our home. We were running across the compound rather than being sensible and walking.

Our old night guard did not recognize who it was and just saw two figures flying past him. He was onto us as thieves and chased us with his bow and arrow. It was a close call, nearly shooting us as we disappeared around the corner calling his name! 'Baba, Baba, it's us don't shoot." He has always been a good night guard. Even now, though he's moving on in years, I wouldn't want to cross him in a dark alley or a dark compound for that matter.

What he is most famous for is his storytelling. On special days, you can get him to sit down and spin a yarn, mostly of when he was young working in the mines in Zimbabwe. His best story and our favourite is the one where he fled the war and walked halfway across the continent to Malawi. He lived on berries and roots, walked at night and rested during the day. It took him six weeks to get here, arriving with just the shirt on his back. He talks about the miracles of the people who'd helped him along the way, of one special missionary woman who gave him medicine to heal the swelling in his legs.

When we first heard this story, we were doubtful. It sounded too unrealistic, the tall stories of imagination let loose. However every time we've heard it repeated, more details come to light. Tim and I cross-referenced when he unpacked the story one more time. The details were exact and the more we asked questions the more realistic it sounded and the more ignorant we felt.

Myself having never walked across even one country let alone several, and my best ever hike lasting a whopping 3 days. I was the gringo, listening to the master, a mere child wide-eyed and lacking in understanding. The story continued with details of what berries to eat and what not to touch, of hunger and the fear of being lost, how to use the stars to guide you and how to stay away from villages and possible trouble on the roads. How your legs swell after a while and the pain associated.

The climax came one night. As usual, he tied himself up the tree so he could sleep safely off the ground without falling out. It took me a while to understand this part. Why not sleep on the ground? (Yes I know nothing!) You see you tie yourself up high in a tree, so the wild animals cannot get you. Most dangerous animals in Africa can't climb trees, hyenas, wild dogs, elephants, hippos etc. with the exception of the most obvious one. You know this when I sat there staring at him, mind completely blank. See, I told you how ignorant a girl from Australia is. What was the most obvious one? The most dangerous animal? I had no idea! What a koala? Maybe a dingo?

He woke up one night face to face to what he thought was a lion! Yikes, can you imagine that! Tied high up in a tree face to face with a lion. (They can climb trees if you didn't know and this makes them even more dangerous.) At this point in the story, he always begins his jolly belly laugh. The one that makes you happy even if you have no idea what he's talking about.

"You wouldn't believe it," He says, "just when I thought I was going to have to fight for my life or die, I realized that I'd made a mistake." He chuckles again. "It wasn't a lion, it was a (insert here the Yawo word used for monkey)."

We would all laugh in relief as he then went on to explain how God had his life in his hands and his time wasn't up. "There I was in the dark face to face with a monkey thinking it was a lion." More laughter. Then he'd shake his head smiling, and fade away into his own memories.

At our dinner table, we would debate whether he meant a baboon or a monkey. Monkeys were small and not easily confused as a lion, but a baboon could be much more aggressive, especially the big ones.

We actually asked him about it and after his explanation presumed that we were right, a baboon was more likely. We assumed, now that we lived in Africa, that we were such knowledgeable experts!

Well, that has been the story for all these years, the baboon that can scare you half to death. It was all very entertaining, but not that unusual, we see baboons all the time. No one really likes them because they destroy the crops and make a nuisance of themselves. However, this story doesn't end here.

As you know, even if you have heard a story a hundred times, that doesn't mean you know all the details. Perhaps it was because over the years our language has kept getting better and we are able to pick up more details and nuances. We thought we knew it all, until tonight. Tim came bounding into the kitchen. " You wouldn't believe what I found out?"

When Tim asks such questions, it is rhetorical. Don't ever try to guess.

"You know the lion that really was a monkey." We know this story so well, I actually knew exactly what he was talking about. " Well, turns out it wasn't a baboon after all. A few of us were discussing the story again tonight when we asked about what the 'monkey' looked like.

Baba had explained more details. "It sounded like a lion, it was really big, much bigger than a man, and it was black, with no hair on its chest, they live near the thick jungle near the Congo border."   That is one strange kind of baboon. After hearing the whole description, this thing was no monkey or even a baboon. Struggling for the English word it came out weird and wrong. He stood up and acted out how this thing walked on its hind legs, huge arms hanging down by its sides.

Tim had taken a sudden gasp of breath when he put two and two together. "Hang on a minute, what? You were woken, tied up in a tree, sitting face to face with a gorilla?" Baba clicked his fingers, excited to hear the English word pronounced properly after all these years.

"Yes, that's it. A gorilla." Tim sat there wide-eyed and dumbfounded with our night guard slapping his leg and erupting again into his jolly old belly laugh. "You see God was looking after me then and he looking after me still now, with him I have nothing to fear."   All Tim could do was nod his head in agreement. "Yisenene!" (Yes indeed!)

CPSIA information can be obtained
at www.ICGtesting.com
Printed in the USA
FSHW020100140820
72937FS